FLASHBACKS

EUROPEAN ETHNOLOGICAL RESEARCH CENTRE
CELTIC & SCOTTISH STUDIES
UNIVERSITY OF EDINBURGH
27-29 GEORGE STREET
EDINBURGH EH8 9LD

D1147209

1. Portrait of George Taylor (date unknown).

FLASHBACKS

From Kelso to Kalamazoo

The Life and Times of George Taylor
1803–1891

Edited by:
Margaret Jeary and Mark A. Mulhern

in association with

THE EUROPEAN ETHNOLOGICAL RESEARCH CENTRE
AND NMS ENTERPRISES LIMITED – PUBLISHING
NATIONAL MUSEUMS SCOTLAND

GENERAL EDITOR
Alexander Fenton

Published in Great Britain in 2009 by
NMS Enterprises Limited – Publishing
NMS Enterprises Limited
National Museums Scotland
Chambers Street, Edinburgh EH1 1JF

Text © Gerald C. Reynolds II/
European Ethnological Research
Centre 2009

Images: all photographs
© as credited 2009

ISBN 978-1-905267-27-9

**British Library Cataloguing in
Publication Data**
A catalogue record of this book
is available from the British Library.

Cover design by Mark Blackadder.
Cover photograph: Portrait of George
Taylor (© Gerald C. Reynolds II)
over detail from Map of Roxburgh-
shire by J. Thomson & Co., 1820
(© Trustees of the National Library
of Scotland).
Internal text design by NMSE –
Publishing, NMS Enterprises
Limited.
Printed and bound in Great Britain
by Athenaeum Press Ltd,
Gateshead, Tyne & Wear.

For a full listing of related
titles please visit:
www.nms.ac.uk/books
www.celtscot.ed.ac.uk/EERC

CONTENTS

ACKNOWLEDGEMENTS

IT has been possible to publish this account only because it has survived since having been written, so thanks must be recorded to George Taylor and his descendents for having taken such good care of his memoir. In particular, Gerald C. Reynolds II is to be thanked for bringing this manuscript to the attention of the editors and for supplying many of the illustrations. The work by Wesley Reynolds and Marcy Wells of preparing the initial typescript was of invaluable assistance to the editors.

Thanks are also recorded to the Department of Horticulture at Michigan State University for confirming the details of George Taylor's essays on horticulture that were published by the Michigan State Horticultural Society.

EDITORIAL NOTE

THE approach taken by the editors has been to preserve, as far as possible, the form and layout of the memoir as given by George Taylor himself. Mr Taylor has used American and British conventions of spelling, and this mixed form of spelling has been preserved. In addition, Mr Taylor has varied the spelling of certain terms such as personal and place names. This variation has been preserved as this work seeks to be an accurate presentation of the original hand-written memoir. Where misspellings may have caused dubiety, they have been corrected by the editors – those changes being indicated by being placed in square brackets. In addition, ellipses are filled by giving missing words in square brackets and additional information, such as State names, is also given in square brackets.

Mark A. Mulhern
EUROPEAN ETHNOLOGICAL RESEARCH CENTRE

LIST OF ILLUSTRATIONS

INTRODUCTION

G EORGE Taylor started to write these memoirs in the early part of 1885. His long life story provides a wonderful examination of the varied spectrum of the life and work in nineteenth-century Lowland Scotland, with a tale of emigration and a more distant land for good measure. Taylor's story seems at once both typical and quite remarkable. Taylor's memoir has its fair share of 'melancholy incidents' which were so often poignantly reported by nineteenth-century newspapers.

The United States of America to which Taylor emigrated was rapidly expanding, hungrily demanding and requiring an increasing number of new people as the new nation opened up. Taylor emigrated to the USA in 1855, the first year of a quinquennium which witnessed an average figure of just over 4000 Scots heading to this destination each year. The 1850s were also a pivotal decade in Scotland's demographic history, particularly as the USA had started to eclipse Canada as the destination *par excellence* for Scottish emigrants; although this was also a period marked by the distinctive yet temporary phenomenon of Australasia attracting the largest proportion of those leaving Scotland for overseas destinations. Taylor's memoir also provides an insight into the close world of the Scottish diaspora. In one incident a friend from Scotland, whom he thought had emigrated to Australia, turns up in Kalamazoo!

Taylor's model of emigration was very typical of that of Lowlanders who frequently embarked from Scotland in search of a more individualistic odyssey with a determined aim to improve themselves and their families. This was in contrast to the more community-based model of the Highland emigration, where emigrants tended to join established diaspora communities, which often replicated social networks from a defined geographic area in the home country. It is also significant that Taylor was an experienced professional nurseryman. Although he left a society which was essentially rural, the nature of his working background serves to underscore the point that most Scots leaving for the USA in the last half of the nineteenth century could be considered as 'skilled'. In the same sense he was a fairly typical Scottish entrant to the 'Land of the Free'.

Taylor also emigrated in an era when Scots as an entity still exerted an influence on American society and culture. After the early 1860s this phenomenon became increasingly diluted. Indeed a reverse phenomenon was the Scottish experience of the last four decades of the nineteenth century when the ever expanding US economy would turn the tables on Scotland and start to exercise more influence over Scottish industrial and commercial affairs.

The Scottish Borders are often overlooked as a point of departure of Scottish emigrants, but the Borders did experience high rates of emigration concomitant with the ebb and flow of rural life, especially in a region so dominated by the landed elite with their *latifundia*. Taylor's experience defines that wonderful phrase coined in the early years of the twentieth century that 'the Scots are notoriously migratory'.

Taylor's incipient political awareness is axiomatic of the Seceder brand of Scottish presbyterianism in which he was raised. T. C. Smout records the comments of Ramsay of Ochtertyre, who noticed that it was the members of the anti-burger Kirk who were the first to refrain from raising their bonnets to the local lairds and their ilk in an incipient display of egalitarianism.

Convinced of the necessity of a more proactive mode of evangelisation, Taylor was convinced that the Evangelical Union was the church for him. This was a congregational denomination founded by the Rev. James Morison, a minister who had been suspended by the United Secession Church for his view on the limits of Calvinism in general and predestination in particular. Taylor's strong Christian ideology of equality is readily evidenced in the numerous comments about his abomination of slavery, long before he adopted American citizenship and espoused the cause of the north in the American Civil War.

It is interesting that despite his close family connections with the United States, and perhaps not least the personal tragedies that affected him, it takes until 1855 for Taylor to finally act on his 'intention to come out to America'. He was then 52 years of age, considerably older than the average age of most emigrants – it was generally an activity for the younger members of society. Much is made in popular history of the involuntary nature of emigration of those who left Scotland, and close connections are drawn between forced clearance and emigration. More recent works on the historical experience of the Scottish emigrant, particularly Marjory Harper's *Adventurers and Exiles,* draws out the fact that many Scots went voluntarily, making informed conscious decisions about the future for the betterment of themselves and their families.

Taylor's experience balances up this narrative. He struck out to the New World with a sense of confidence and self-belief so many Scots must have possessed as they too embarked on their voyage of discovery. Comparing his own character and prospects with that of his brothers who had gone to the USA so many years before, he opined that, 'I had surely a good if not better chance than they'. Although the New York-built *John Bright* was a brand new vessel, Taylor's shipboard reminiscences brings home the trials and tribulations of the emigrant journey. Even in the middle years of the nineteenth century, both the elements and effects of illness and disease continued to dictate the conditions of passage.

As expected, there is much comment from Taylor about his work as a gardener and nurseryman. True to the innovative tradition of the Scots at home and especially abroad, he was responsible for the introduction of the commercial cultivation of celery to the USA. However, at times in his memoirs the minutiae of his business affairs overwhelm the great events of his family life. His third wife's death from a tuberculosis-related disease is squeezed quite literally between the description of his purchase of a stock of plants and an account of how he was able to add to the overall size of his nursery.

One of the notable features of Taylor's narrative as it develops is the change in his vocabulary and emphasis which charts his transformation from a Scot to a fully-fledged American. That true Americanism 'gotten' creeps into his language. By the time of his trip home to Scotland in 1862, he celebrates the efficiency of the American check system in railway travel, while bemoaning the need to push through the crowd to retrieve his luggage, a symptom of the inefficient system of the old country.

Taylor's adopted city of Kalamazoo changed dramatically from the moment of his arrival to the time that he eventually committed his interesting memoirs to paper in 1885. When Taylor first settled in Kalamazoo it was a community with a population of around 3000. By the time he had finished composing his *Memoir*, Kalamazoo had already been legally incorporated as a city, and the number of its citizens was fast approaching 17,000. Positioned half-way between Chicago and Detroit, Kalamazoo became an important railway junction in western reaches of Michigan. It is no surprise that Taylor makes such frequent use of Michigan's well-placed railway system for his various trips.

It is the way in which Taylor can range from the everyday to items of national and historical import that make his text so compelling. Coming from Kalamazoo, his pro-Union and anti-slavery comments on the American Civil War are quite pertinent. Indeed Kalamazoo was the only venue in the state of Michigan where Lincoln made a speech during the conflict between the states.

Taylor's narrative began with the story of his own mother and father's emigration to the USA at the very start of the nineteenth century in 1802. This migratory autobiography ends with the writer taking stock and reflecting on his own life and position on the eve of the last decade of that same century. Despite many personal tragedies, Taylor's account of his life and times, written at the great age of 86, is a rich and intriguing example of what one might term a Scottish 'success story' – an experience shared by so many Scots who left their homeland during this era of mass migration.

David S. Forsyth, 2009
NATIONAL MUSUEMS SCOTLAND

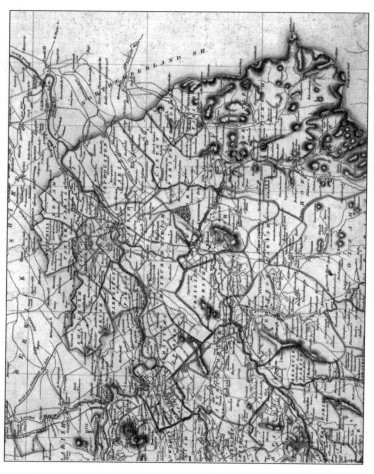

2. Map of the north of Roxburghshire (1832) [detail].

FROM KELSO TO KALAMAZOO

I

Early Life

I HAVE no further genealogy of my ancestors than that of grandfathers and grandmothers on both sides. So far as I can ascertain, they were of the Scottish Border among the Cheviots in the county of Roxburgh.

I was once favored to make some extracts from an old Record of a Book belonging to the Secession Church at Morebattle, where I found a list of *Births*, *Marriages*, and *Baptisms* of three generations.

I learned from this Record that my ancestors did not belong to the Established Church, but must have been devoted followers of Boston and the Erskines. They seemed also to have belonged to the working class and have to earn their daily bread by farm labor.

From this Register I found that my father, Andrew Taylor, was the son of George Taylor and Mary Common, who were married on the 21st of January 1763. My father was born at Grange in the Parish of Hownam on the 25th of September 1768. Then I found on my mother's side, that Alexander, son of Alexander Stevenson and Mary Wright, was born on the 20th of February 1781.

My father was a shepherd on a large farm on the Bowmont called Attonburn. It was the custom on some of those large farms for the shepherds and the other single servants to board at the farmhouse. It was in this capacity that my mother and father got acquainted, she being kitchen maid or cook for the whole household.

The record of their marriage is:

> Married Andrew Taylor and Violet Stevenson, 6th of
> April 1801. David Morrison, Minister, George Bell and
> Alexander Stevenson, Witnesses.

They went right away to America and sailed from Greenock
with the ship *Franklin* on the 26th of April and landed at New
York on the 16th of June, a passage of six weeks and three days.
Their passage money was for steerage 14 Guineas and to find
their own victuals, and they were bound to lay in a supply for
10 weeks. They were kindly entertained on board by the Captain
and had upon the whole a good passage.

They went up the Hudson to Albany and from there to Cherry
Valley [Illinois] on the *Mohawk*, where they remained until the
month of May. My mother's health was poorly and so they resolved to come home again.

I have a receipt of their passage by two of the agents on the
1st of May 1802 for the sum of 56 dollars or 12 Guineas from
New York to Greenock by the Ship *George*, Donald Campbell
Master. Then they came home again, and I see from certain docu-
ments that my Father had sole management of Attonburn till the
end of the lease, the Farmer A. Wmn. Andrew Pringle having
died since he left.

Such then is a little of my Ancestral History. I see from the
Secession Book that I was born at Grange in the Parish of Hownam on the 12th of February 1803. I suppose that was where
my grandmother was living, she having been left a widow for
some time previous.

The first place where I looked upon the world and was cap-
able of remembering anything was at the farm of Currburn in
the Parish of Morebattle at the foot of the Cheviots.

My father had engaged to be shepherding there, and was four
years in that place. I was over five years old when my Father left
that place and I found afterwards that I had quite a distinct recol-
lection of the place and the surrounding scenery. There were
pretty steep hills both behind and in front. A little wild wimpling

Burn ran close by and on[e] of the first objects that struck my attention was [a] large tree close upon the bank and at the end of the Burn. And there is one thing I recollect in this connection about a Foxhunt. [Reynard] had been hard pursued and he leaped upon a stone wall built to the side of the barn. From this he sprang to the thatch and up the slope roof to the top, where he lay undiscovered for some time. At last was seen and was forced to leap down and again being pursued by the hounds, and was captured in a little while.

I recollect distinctly about sheep washing and sheep shearing and the Threshing of grain with the flail, and here in this connection I met with a new sensation. They had brought a Fanning Machine, which I had never seen before, and were making preparations to fan a heap of oats that had been threshed as I was looking on. And as they began to put the Machine in operation, the noise that it made, the movement of the wheels, the wind, and the cloud of dust that rose up—all together so unexpected, quite overwhelmed me with fear. I took to my heels and ran into the house to my Mother in the greatest state of excitement; after she had calmed my fear, I could go and look with pleasure at this operation.

There was one trait of character that was early manifested in me, and that was a love of books with pictures. My Mother used to relate how I once gave her a fright in this way. In all those Country Houses it was necessary to have two large Box Beds. These were set on each side of the house, leaving a space, the breadth of a door betwixt them: this formed two apartments, which were known in Scotland by the terms of a But and a Ben. In these Beds of ours, there was a wooden shelf at both the head and the foot, where Books or any other choice article could be placed. My father had a collection of books on these shelves, and one he had lately got was: *Three Hundred Animals*. They were all pictured with description of character, beginning with the lion and ending with a lower grade. I was much interested with this and some other of the books that had pictures. And so it happened that I climbed into the bed and was for a time quietly enjoying the pictures. My Mother, on looking around both outside and in, could not find me. A suspicious thought struck her, as she had several times before seen me go down to the Burn and watch with interest the trout and minnows sporting in the pools and eddies of that little stream.

The thought that I might have fallen in and got drowned put her into a state of excitement, and so she ran so far up and so far down, and nothing of me was to be seen; she then came back to the house in an awful state of suspense, when she thought she had heard something stirring in the bed. When on looking in, there was I as busy among the books as a sage in his study.

The farm buildings and shepherds houses are all isolated and scattered at considerable distances from each other in these Districts. The hills often run in oblong ranges and are beautifully rounded off and covered with a fine smooth crop of the best pasturage. The shepherds often meet each other on the hills, and are social and kindly in their family visits.

As everything we see only appears great or little, or a novelty by comparison, so I found this to be the case on my first visit away from home. This was to the village of Yetholm, which stands about three miles below Bowmont. I never had seen a building larger than a Thatched Cottage, and on looking on a range of buildings, two or three stories high, standing opposite each other, with the shop and their various wares for sale, these novelties altogether seemed to me exceedingly great.

I recollect also that there were certain visitors that called around upon us. One of these was the Gypsy Class. They ostensibly traveled for the sale of Crockery Ware, Horn Spoons, and some other odds and ends. They also collected rags with which they were ready to barter for their own wares. Their mode of transit for business was the Cuddie and Creel. Their women did all the trading, leaving the men and the Cuddies at a distance, while they with a large basket of crockery on their arm and with on[e] or two ragged hungry-looking children following, they came into the house without any ceremony asking: "Now Mistress, what are gan to want in or [a]way the day."

They were persevering in showing off their different wares: and then came an inquiry for rags. If a trade was made, there was a good deal more than they were willing to take. But trade or not, they were always hungry: and especially the children who had hardly broken their fast that day. Such was the way in which they combine their trade with begging. But we knew that they were also great thieves; for if there were any clothes drying, or any loose things lying around, they were apt to stick to their fingers.

There was another class that used to call round at regular intervals—Peddler or Packman, as he was generally called. Some of these dealt in software in all sorts of Cotton Linens, and Woolen fabrics. These Packmen were generally good talkers and very communicative: and as they traveled over an extensive district, they were well [provided] with all the Local News. And as there were a few newspapers at the time, they could often relate some of the last great exploits of Napoleon Bonaparte. There were certain of the Shepherds' Houses where these Peddlers regularly stopped all night, where they had a good Crack and a mutual entertainment. In the morning after breakfast, some nice trinket was presented to the mistress, which often led to a greater purchase from the peddler.

There was also another class that sometimes came round, and that was the regular Beggers in the early part of the Reign of George the Third. The old soldiers had no pensions: and I have seen some of them going about in this way, some without Arm and some on Crutches without a Leg, and some of these frequently had a Medal authorizing them to beg. I recollect of hearing a case related in the last Century which took place at the Caverton Edge Race Course about three miles from Kelso.[1] There was an old Soldier of the name of Andrew Gemmels, who had served in some of the great wars in Germany, and who had been traveling with his Meal Bags all over the country. He was attending the races, where there was always a great crowd of people. There was also a recruiting party to enlist Soldiers, [and as] was common in such cases, the party marched through the crowd with Fife and Drum and a great display. When a halt was called and the recruiting officer had come forward and made a grand speech exalting the honor and the glory of the Soldiers, Old Gemmels came prominently forward in the middle of the crowd, and holding up his Meal Bags cried, "Behold The End Of It".

All that beggar class whether men or women were as a matter of business ragged and dirty: in this way they often got a supply of better clothing, but when it was thought too good, it was sold and turned into money. And so some of the characters have been known to have left a good sum of money at their deaths. This system of open begging has now been nearly done away with in both Scotland and England. In many of the parishes there is a poor rate of fund provided for any of the resident poor who from age and not having any relations able to support them are allowed from this fund a weekly supply. Within the last fifty years ... extensive emigrations has done something to relieve this poverty, but in many cases the root of the evil will exist so long as the drinking usages in these countries are continued.

I recollect of another traveling class who were sort of weekly visitors and were known by the name of Cadgers. Their principal business was to buy and collect eggs from both the farmers and their hinds and cotters who kept a great many chickens. Some of these traveled with a horse and cart and had various merchandise for sale, such as: tea, sugar, snuff, and tobacco. Other of these had cuddy and creel which consisted of two large square wicker boxes, strapped together and suspended on each side, frequently a rider might be sitting on the middle with a leg on each side.

Three cadgers came around every week on a certain day; for they studied to avoid each other—and hence arose the old Scotch Saying, "That there is aye ill will among Cadgers". And here necessarily came in a division of Labor. These eggs and other produce, which they gathered, had to be taken to some Town or City for sale. This was often the special business of some other member of the family, who went to Edinburgh or Berwick with what had been previously collected, sold them there and purchased and brought home all that was necessary for their country trade. But now all this sort of business has been greatly changed since the railroad had become the great medium of transportation.

I may here mention that my father removed from the Farm of Currburn, where he had been shepherd four years to the Farm of Hoselaw Bank in the parish of Linton on the 28th of May, 1808. And before entering into my personal history here, I think it necessary in the first place to give a little sketch of the relation in which the farmer stands to the landlords and then in what relation the laborers stand to the farmer.

In the first place then it is a fact that a few great landlords possess the greater part of all the land in Scotland, England, and Ireland. And to secure these estates from being divided at the decease of the proprietors, they are all entailed—a legal act by which a property cannot be divided but must be inherited by one heir. Only moveable property is subject to division. These lands are divided into farms, and on these a good house is built for the farmer and adjacent are all the necessary farm buildings, so placed, as to form an inclosed square where the various grades of cattle are stalled and fed. Then there is another class of building for the plowmen and other laborers on the farm. The farms are in turn divided into fields by fencing. Now then after these farms are thus equipped they are advertised to be let to a tenant for a certain number of years (generally 19) on certain conditions and at specified rent per annum. The advertisement mentions the name of the farm, the number of acres, and that offers will be received by a party up to a certain date. Then may be seen different parties riding and walking over the farm carefully examining the land and fences with all the various buildings. The mode of giving in the bid is sometimes keen competition for a good farm and it is at the option of the landlord whether he may accept the highest bidder or not. One that is possessed of good capital is often the one that is preferred.

There is another law which these landlords have got up to favor themselves and is called the Law of Hypothec, and it works somewhat in this way: If a farmer would fall behind in the payments of his rent for one or two years, the landlord could seize all of his moveable property, and if he is owing a large bill to the manure merchant or seedman, grocer, dry goods merchant, or any other man, none of these can touch a thing until the landlord is fully paid. And this, in many cases, he takes all and the other creditors receive nothing. The farmer upon taking the farm, must furnish it with stock horses, plough, and all other agricultural implements. He must engage the plowman and other laborers to work the land, and also shepherd. The engagement of these workers is generally for one year, the term being the 26th of May Whitsunday. For the single servant women or men connected with the farmhouse or those who engage as workers with the plowman or shepherds, their engagement is for half year from Whitsunday to 22nd of November. Thus, I have given a sketch of the mode of rural life in Scotland, and it will be seen that many of them are really the servant of servants and are dependent on others, yet it is wonderful how happy many of them are, and as Burns says, "[An' buirdly] Chiels and clever Hizzies are bred in sic a way as this."

I now come back to where my father engaged to be a shepherd with a James Burn on the Farm of Hos[e]law Bank. I here entered upon a new field with some scenery and some new sensations. The flitting, as it was called in taking down the wooden box beds, the press, the dishes, with all the plates, the bowls. Everything were masses in confusion and packed on the carts was quite a sensation.

I recollect my grandmother, whose maiden name was Mary W[r]ight took me in charge to walk with her, and I mind the walk well. It was first down the burn to the Bowmont and then down to Yetholm. We then called at the House of William Stobs,

3. View of Hoselaw. George Taylor's father worked at
Hoselaw Bank farm as a shepherd.

SOURCE: MARGARET AND PETER JEARY

who was one of the weekly Cadgers that came round and were
very kindly entertained. This was the first of three miles of our
journey and we had another three miles to go. We now made our
way across the Hough of Bowmont, then up a steep hill and close
by the shepherds' dwelling, called the Breakhouse. Then still up
and along the side of some stone dykes. We kept winding around
till we saw before us a little farm hamlet by the name of Wide-
open. After passing this, we began to march downhill; and then
a little to the west we saw at a distance the place of our destination, on this was a farm house of the old style with Barn Byreshed
and two dwelling houses, forming a sort of a square. These buildings stood on a ridge of old pasture and running to a point—on
the north was a lake, or [Loch], as they called it, of about thirty
acres. To the west was an extensive Mop [Moss], where a great
many Peats had been and were still being cut out. This was called
the Dun [Moss], as the Peat was of a brownish dun color. Then on
the south side, the [Moss] stretched in a sort of oblong form to

the east. This Mop was a soft black and easily cut, and the peats, when dried, were hard and burnt finely. They were indeed our principle fuel. The name of this old place was called Loch-inches—I suppose from its position between the [Loch] and the Mop. There was a connection with the Hos[e]law Bank Farm, and our house was here, as most of the pastureland lay in this direction. There were three families living here, besides ours.

My father and another family lived in the old farmhouse and the others in two cottage houses, joined together. They were all oldish people that lived here, so that I had no boys to associate with. But I found much to interest me in some other things about it. In the [Loch] there was a little island, where hundreds of white fowl, called the Pick Maw, used to come in the spring and make their nests. They laid three light blue eggs and were thought good eating. I was in the way of gathering a great many of them, both for the neighbors, and ourselves. There were also a good many wild ducks that used to make their nests about this Mop and [Loch]. One of these nests with a dozen or more of fresh eggs was a good prize. There were certain kinds of berries that grew in this Mop, of which I gathered a good many. The best of these was the Cranberry. It was of the same species as our Americans of that name, but much smaller, though I think the quality was equally good. In the season I used to gather a great many of these and could readily sell them for a shilling per bottle or quart. I may say that the blueberry ... used to grow on the dry knolls among the heather. They are a species of our huckleberry in taste and color, but not quite large. There was another little black species, which grew on a hard, wiry stem, which was known by the name of the crawberry. It was pretty good eating, but not equal to others.

The farm of Hos[e]law Bank as the road winded round the East End of the [Loch], was about ¾ of a mile from our house. They kept three pair of workhorses on the farm. But the greater part was native pastures, so that a good many of both sheep and cattle were kept. Some of the land was not fenced, and that required a herding of the sheep and cattle, to keep them from eating the grain.

Hos[e]law Bank, as the name indicates, stood on a ridge of high ground, running east and west. From this could be seen to the north of the whole of Berwickshire for a distance of 20 miles in a north and east direction. There was one thing from which I derived great pleasure in this landscape views, and that was from a small telescope, which my father had recently got. He showed me how to fix and adjust the lens. With this instrument, objects that were 12 or 20 miles distant appeared distinct and quite near. I could see the old Hume Castle with many of the prominent gentlemen seats, the town of Coldstream, and the bridge across the Tweed appeared very fine, especially when the afternoon sun shone upon it. Windmills for threshing the grain had become quite a rage at that time. With this glass I could count as many as 20 and could often see them moving. By this amusement the weary listlessness of herding was greatly taken away.

The season of harvest was then a matter of interest to all parties, both young and old (old and young). To the men and women it was hard work, as the cutting or shearing, as they called it, was all done with a savor teeth hook. Not only did all the men and women on the farm take a part in this work, but also the trades-people of the town and village were all prepared to engage in this work. The rate of harvest wages at that time was from 12 to 15 shillings per week with victuals and lodging. The length of time was often a month and sometimes more. The farmer furnished the victuals. This consisted of oatmeal porridge in the morning. It was brought out to the field about eight o'clock in bowls or wooden vessels with hoops, having the capacity to hold porridge for 7 persons. This was called a Bandwin, which consisted of 6 shearers and one bandster, to bind and set up what was cut. These bowls being set down on the Stubble at proper distances from each other. Each company following their Bandster, surrounded the vessel, either setting themselves down on their knees, or lying broadside on and with spoon in hand. The first move was to dig out a hole in the dish, so that when a tin of milk was poured on, in the center of each hole would be in the way of receiving a certain amount.

This, I know, would rather look Hoggish in the eyes of our American Citizen, but being the custom of the country, there was nothing for it, but to accept the situation. Moreover great many of these people had been up Three Hours and had now a Splendid Appetite. When an hour had passed, work was again resumed and continued till One o'clock, when Dinner was brought out. This consisted of a loaf of bread and a quart of beer to each person. The Brewer especially prepared this beer for the Harvest and made engagement with the farmer to deliver it for so much a Barrel. The dinner hour over, the same work goes on till 6 o'clock, which then, makes a day of ten hours work. Then [m]ake their way for home. When at the Farm House the[y] find the supper waiting with the same fare as in the morning—good Oatmeal Porridge and Milk.

I have thus given the whole bill of Harvest Fare and some may think it is a very mean one, but I can speak from what I have seen and also from what I have experienced, that the hardest work can be done and the best of health enjoyed on just such a fare. But now this mode of work is greatly a thing of the past. The Reaping Machine has made an entire Revolution in all Harvest work.

Young people enjoyed the Harvest in the olden days. It was the common practice for all the young and also for some old people to gather or glean what was left on the stubble behind the reapers. I used to do a good deal of this work and have a good pile at the end of the harvest. But I recollect I was sometimes necessarily engaged otherwise and had to act a housekeeper at home.

It was then the general custom for all Farm house holders to pay a rent of 50 shillings for the House they occupied or to shear for the House, as they termed it—that is, either the wife or the Servant must shear all the time of Harvest and receive no payment. In that case my Mother did the same as many other mothers—sheared all through the harvest and saved 50 shillings. In that case, being the oldest, I had to keep House and take care of the younger members of the family. And I can well recollect that one Harvest (it must have been 1812) I had to carry out the youngest to be nursed by his Mother at Breakfast and Dinner hours. This is only a sample of the way in which Women, and especially mothers are subjected under the say of a wealthy Landed Aristocracy.

When I look at the poverty, oppression, and suffering which I have seen flowing from this source, I cannot but think that the language and utterance of the Epistle of James in Chapter 5 and say of the rich man: "Behold the hire of the laborers who have reaped down your fields which is of you kept back by fraud crieth, and the cries of them which have reaped are entered into the ears of the Lord of Sabbath—Your riches shall eat your flesh as fire!"

Our neighbors in this old hamlet at Lochinches were all religious, god-fearing people, but they all went to different churches. I recollect it was common practice in the Sabbath afternoon, to gather at one of the houses and talk over what had been hearing at their various churches. The texts of their ministers were mentioned and some of the leading remarks of the sermon. Sometimes a sermon or a portion of some good book was read and altogether they showed a great regard for the sanctity of the Sabbath. Family worship was also regularly observed in all of these families. The ministers were also attentive in visiting round among their members, and it was then the practice in every alternate year to have what they called a Diet of Examination. This was generally held in a certain district and a notice of it was given at the church on the previous Sabbath.

The people having thus met at a certain appointed place, the exercises were begun with singing and prayer, then a shorter catechism question was asked at each member all round. It was generally understood that everyone should be well posted on the questions, as it was one of the first things taught in both the home and the school. After this, the minister asked a series of scripture questions at each one in order, adapting them in a certain way to each individual capacity. There were always a few who were more deeply read in the scriptures and Divinity. These had harder questions asked, so as to bring the truth more fully to their weaker brethren. The children and young people were not overlooked, but had also questions. The established church had then also Diets of Examination, but these now I believe with both parties are on things of the past.

My grandmother was a frequent visitor at our house. She had a house and home of her own at Morebattle, but went frequently round among her family relations. Her family consisted of three: her oldest son, Alexander Stevenson was married to Agnes Nibbit and had a family of one daughter and four sibs and was shepherd at Cessford. Her next daughter, Agnes was married to John Mable, who was also a shepherd. They had three sons and two daughters, and after moving from place to place came out to America in 1818. My mother, Violet, was the youngest, and had a family of eight—five sons and three daughters.

It was remarked that I was a great favorite with my grandmother, and I had often to go home with her to Morebattle, and when there, I had to go round with her in a visit to a great many of her acquaintances. There were a great many weavers in that town. Four of these by the name of Craig were all friends but had all separate families. In visiting these, I was very much interested to see them working on their looms. It was something entirely new to me, and showed how our shirts and other clothing were made. And here I may mention what an immense amount of labor we then had with this article flax. We had first to go to market, buy seed, and bring it home. Then there was a day when it had to be sown. As it came up and grew, a weakening process had to be gone through. When it was ripe, it had to be pulled up and tied in beets or bunches. Then it had to be steeped in water for ten days: then spread thinly out and lie on the ground about a month. Then tied up and taken under cover. Then there was a breaking and pounding process. The next was the manual process of what they called swingling. All the wives helping each other in due order. This being done, it was all ready for the final and last process—the heckler or flax dresser, who put it in bundles ready for the spinning wheel. After the spinning, then the reeling into hanks and slips, when finally it was ready to be taken to the weaver. Then when he in his loom has wrought it into a web of shirting, he brings it home rolled up on his back. Next, he measures it out with his yardstick, and the bill of payment is made out at so much per yard. Still it is not ready to be cut for a shirt. It has to undergo a process of bleaching: and the place for this is near a supply of water, where it is spread out. And there it is alternately wetted and dried for two or three weeks. When finally it is pronounced finished, rolled up, put away in the clothes press, and frequently shown to visitors as a fine piece of Sarking. I have given this extensive process in the order as I have seen or done a part of it myself.

When at Morebattle with my grandmother, I had always to go with her to the meeting house on the Sabbath day. Possible at the time I was more interested with some of the external surroundings than the preaching of old David Morrison. All the meeting houses at that time were built and constructed in a very plain style. I suppose their object was to steer as far as possible from that of the Catholic or Episcopal. As their forefathers had suffered a good deal of persecution from both of those parties.

This old meeting house was of an oblong form, and no doubt was considered as stylish for its day as it had a slated roof. The walls were of equal height all round, and the roof at the ends were stopped to the wall. There was a gallery in front and at both ends, the pulpit and windows occupying one side. These pulpits were also a little peculiar. They were of a box and formed a seat behind for two and a little sloping desk before the Bible and Psalm book. They stood high, having a stair leading up to them. Down below this in front was the Precentor's seat and desk that lead the singing. This was then quite an arduous matter, as he had to read out every line in a sort of musical tone before it was sung. There were no hymns sung then: it was all the Psalms of David.

My grandmother's seat in this house was on one of the side galleries. The way of entering was from the outside by a sloping ascent to a door at the top of the wall, from which there was way of access to all of the seats. There was a similar construction at the end of the house for an entrance to the galleries on that side.

* * *

In that pastoral district a great many of those attending were shepherds, many of them had their dogs with them, and the most of these dogs seemed to know that they were in a sacred place and behaved well, though more than once I have seen a little bit of a dog fight. One thing that interested me was when the people rose at the pronouncing of the blessing. The dogs seemed to know where they were at, and at once made a rush for the door and down the grade before the service was finished. I have since read a Scotch anecdote, which verifies my observation. In a rural district, a stranger minister had been preaching one Sabbath. When he arose to pronounce the blessing he seemed surprised when the people sat still. Then an old shepherd seemed to comprehend the situation and rose up and thus addressed the minister: "Oh sir, just say away: we sit still to cheat the dogs."

There was another peculiar feature with certain parties attending these meetings. Many of the farmers and those whom had horses used to ride to church, and on taking their wives and other lady friends, they were in the way of riding double. This was done by girding on a separate seat or pad, as they called it, behind the saddle. This was the form in which many of the farmers rode with their wives to church and market. Burns, the poet, alludes to this when speaking of different parties on their way to church:

"Farmers rash in riding graith gaed haddin by their cotties."[2]
Such now are all things of the past.

These church meetings were at that time a kind of social in
their way in the summertime, when the days were long. There
was always an interval of an hour between forenoon and afternoon services. There was a fine piece of smooth lawn grass on the
south side of the church, where might be seen at that time, scores
of little parties sitting or lying on the grass, eating a piece of bread
and cheese, or some other refreshment they had brought with
them. Here neighbors and acquaintances met, where residences
might be ten or more miles apart, and thus afforded them a good
opportunity for both social and religious intercourse.

My grandmother had always a large party of friends at her
house at the time of these intervals, and I recollect how she was
in the way of preparing for this. She had a large metal pot that
she called the Kalie Pot. This was half or more filled with water.
Cabbages and other vegetables had been all cut and prepared
on Saturday evening (for she was very strict, as to the letter, in
keeping the Sabbath). These with a certain amount of fleshmeat,
pot barley, and salt, were the principle ingredients that filled the
pot. It was set a boiling early and well on by 11 o'clock, the hour
for church. A decent fire was put below and thus left to itself for
an hour and a half. When the church came out, everything in the
pot was in a toothsome order. The plates and horn spoons, the
knives and forks were all set in order—and then was a meal of
real friendly and social intercourse.

I think it was about the end of the year 1810 that I first
entered on my school experience. The nearest place at that time
was at the village of Lempitlaw in the parish of Sprouston. I had
learned the letters of the alphabet early and had primary lessons
from my father and mother, so that I could now read pretty fair
lesson in the New Testament. I recollect my father went with
me and introduced me to the schoolmaster. He was a young man,
I should thin[k] about 18 years of age. His name was Thomas
Scot. This was not a parish school, but was got up for the con-

venience of the village and the surrounding country. This school at that time was held in one of the old-fashioned dwelling houses. It was thatched with upright beams that supported the roof and came down to the walls to the foundation, at the top of the wall. There was a joint with another beam of timber, which slanted up to the top, thus meeting its neighbor on the opposite side and forming the skeleton of the roof. The intervening spaces, being filled up with large, strong branches to support the thatch. The entrance was primitive, being by what they called an outside and an inside door. On entering, there was to the right a clear space of about a rod; the whole breadth of the house close to the left was a partition running through, and at the end was the door of the entrance into the main body of the school. Here, three or four desks set across with some intervening seats between; and there was one seat from the entering of the door, running the whole length along the wall and across to the south side, where were two or three windows.

The entrance porch was very useful for the boys playing tops and marbles. I commenced first with a class reading the New Testament, and then with the Hardies Collection and spelling book. The tasks, which we had to commit to memory, were the shorter catechism and the Psalms of David. But occasionally there were some extras. I recollect that one of my teachers subsequently offered a prize of a new Psalm book to any of the school who would learn and repeat from memory most correctly the 119th Psalm. I was pronounced the successful candidate and was consequently awarded the book.

At another time, by another teacher, the prize of a New Testament was offered for any of the school who would learn and repeat most correctly the three chapters of St. Matthew, which relates the Sermon on the Mount. In this case, I was also successful.

There were several of my first tasks, as they then appeared, were quite form[id]able. My first commencement of writing was one of these, and more especially when I saw before me a fine copper plate as a pattern to write from. And something of the same feeling came over me on my first commencement with arithmetic, when a Table of Enumeration and Multiplication first came before me. It is here that the success of a teacher comes in, presenting a proper method from lower to a higher in all their many and various relations.

One great exciting scene in that period of my life was the attending of certain fairs and markets, as they came around in their season. One of these was the Town Yetholm Lamb Fair on the 5th of July. It was my father's business to take a certain number of lambs to the fair, and this was done by parting very early in the morning. I had always to go with him to help drive and keep them separate among the many others in the market. A great many strangers and to me strange new things were always to be seen: and greater, was the St. James [fair] held on the 5th of August near Kelso. The principle business in the early part of the day was [the] hiring market for Shearers through the course of the Harvest at so much per week with victuals: but it was more a great gathering of Country people, young and old for pleasure and socia[bility]. The Gypsy Class was there with their various wares. Peddlers and Hucksters of all sorts were arranged in long side rows, where a constant stream of people kept walking up and down between them. Here you would have seen a great crowd of listening to a Ballad Singer, and many of these songs at that time were Patriotic. I recollect on old fellow who sang with great energy and the refrain or overwords of the Song was: "And Wellington wiel go wiel go with Wellington, wiel go we will across the Main Ocean and face our daring foe."

There were always a number of shows and other various amusements. But what gave the Fair its chief aspect was the great number of Tents covering the whole ground: their ostensible purpose being to supply eating and refreshments. It was from the last mentioned that those parties derived their profits in the sale of Ale and intoxicating drinks. And as the afternoon and evening drew on, its effects were being manifested by many of the crowd. Fighting was quite common circumstances, and some were inducted to enlist with a recruiting party as soldiers, and their next day on reflection with friends, they were induced to go back and get out of this engagement by paying what they called a Smart of one or two guineas.

These Fairs afforded also a fine opportunity for young men and women meeting together, and having a Swagger, as they called it—joining arm in arm and walking in this way up and down among the crowd. Then as it began to draw toward evening, each young man must take his sweetheart to her home, even though it should be si[x] miles in the opposite direction of his own. In this way certain alliances were often entered upon which in the end had an unpleasant termination.

The market or Hiring days for the services of single men and women for the half years were often attended in much the same way and presented many of the same scenes that I have already described.

* * *

From the time that I was born and 12 years subsequently, Napoleon Bonaparte kept all Europe in a state of war and excitement, even in Great Britain at one time was threatened with invasion. I have heard though I do not remember, about [what] they called The Lightening of Beacons. This was long before the Telegraph was thought of, and was an expedient for the giving of an immediate alarm to the whole country. The plan was to have great lights on all prominent hills twelve miles apart, so that should an invasion take place, an alarm by these lights could be given all over the country in a few minutes. In this order of things there had been a trained Militia of Volunteers to be ready at any emergency. I have heard some amusing stories related of the various effects produced by this alarm on families and individuals, when called at once to march to headquarters and meet the foe. The wailing of wives for their husbands, and mothers for their sons was quite pathetic, but in a few hours afterwards, when it was found to be a hoax, many of the former scenes so very touching, appeared now a little amusing and somewhat ludicrous.

There were a few newspapers in that age, and such as there were greatly taken up with the wars and conquest of Napoleon Bonaparte. My father always contrived in some way to get hold of a newspaper. I frequently brought it, as I came home from school. This he used to read with some of the neighbors in the evening, and I have sometimes listened with their various comments about the War.

I can recollect particularly the thrilling sensation all parties felt when reading an account of the disastrous retreats of Napoleon and his French army from Moscow. This was thought at the time to finish his career, but he was still able to rally for another great campaign.

In 1813 my father made a change of his situation from Hos[e]-law Bank, where he had been for five years to the Farm of [H]ol[e]-field, and so we moved to that place on May 26th. Along with his situation as Shepherd he had also to keep a boy to herd cows and cattle on the farm through the course of the summer half-year. This then was my work till the Martinmas term, 22nd November. This farm was close adjacent to the English Border and I had frequent occasion to be across the line.

In my daily occupation I had a great deal of spare time, and as there ran through the Farm two fine burns or creek, where there were some fine trout, I often caught a number of these in various ways.

I often spent some time in reading when I could get hold of any interesting books, but at this time there were but few books that were got up especially for the use of young people. On the Sabbath days my mother always saw that I had the Bible with me, or some other good religious book. Some of these I read with pleasure and profit. *Heavy Meditations* was one and also by the same author *The Dialogues of Theron and Aspasia*. I think I knew the Scheme of Salvation through the meditation of the Lord

Jesus Christ before this, but the reading of these Dialogues threw
so much light on man as a sinner and Christ as a savior that the
way seemed open and plain.

I can well recollect the very spot of ground where I was reading one Sabbath forenoon and when thinking and praying over
what I had read, I seemed to enter into such a happy confidence
and assurance of Peace and Love of God that I had no fear of
Death, but a certain calm elevation. Above the World it seemed
to me at that time as a sort of First Fruits of the Joy and Peace
of Believing.

I went to school in the winter of 1814. There was a very heavy
snow that season, and the frost was severe about the beginning
of April. I made my first visit to Kelso along with my mother.
This was what the country people called the first Linseed Friday,
when they came to buy seed and have it ready for sowing. I went
to help carry home the seed with other necessities for the house.
A good part of the road was new to me. We crossed the Tweed in
a boat at Sprouston, and this was the first time I had either seen
or sailed in a boat. We then walked two miles up the side of the
river to the Town and in the course of this walk, there were some
fine houses with their surroundings on each side of the river. As
we drew near to the Town we heard the ringing of bells and beating of drums with other Martial music. A great flag could be seen
flying upon the top of the old Cathedral [perhaps Kelso Abbey]
and smaller ones on many of the other buildings. The Town had
just received the news, which is still great in history, and it was
this: "The Allies had entered Paris." Bonaparte was now a prisoner
and caged in his own headquarters.

The Town of Kelso that day with its shops and their various
displays, other buildings, with all their surrounding made altogether such an impression of greatness and grandeur as I had
never seen before.

At the Whitsunday term May 26th 1814, my father again
made a change of situation. To the Farm of Graden in the Parish
of Linton. I sometimes rendered him help with the sheep, but

was for the most part of that summer employed on the Farm in singling and hoeing turnips. These are all cultivated in drills. The most of this and a good deal of the other farm work is done by women.

Each householder had then to furnish a worker whose wages at that time were tenpence a day. I was what they called an extra half worker, and so my wages were in like proportion. In the time of Harvest I had to keep house and take care of the younger members of the family, while my mother had to shear for the house rent. Gleaning in the field was allowed, and I was in the way of bringing out the family, and had often a good pile gathered in the evening.

In the winter half year I went to school at Linton, the distance being fully three miles. The name of the Schoolmaster was Samuel Wilson. He was an oldish man, a Bachelor, and his sister, an Old Maid was his housekeeper. He was a good teacher and the school was crowded; a great many coming from the neighboring parishes. I may say he was the last of my school teachers, and it was under his tuition that I made the most progress in reading, writing, and arithmetic—these being then the only branche[s] taught in the Parish Schools.

My father was two years Shepherd in this place, and I passed the time much in the same way as I have described.

It was in this last year 1815 that Napoleon Bonaparte made his last great struggle for the supremacy in Europe, which culminated with the Battle of Waterloo on the 16th of June. For some time previous, my father and some of the neighbors had been watching and discussing, as to what would be the outcome of the great Military Movement then going on. He got a Kelso Weekly Paper (I think it was the *Mail*) and it always came to hand on the Friday evening and was awaited with anxiety. One of our neighbors, an old woman who was a Cadger and kept a Cuddie and creel, went to Kelso every Friday in the way of business, and also as carrier of the mail to any in the neighborhood.

It was a fine summer evening, about eight o'clock, when old

Peggy Vine and her Cuddie arrived. The paper was at once handed out and opened by my father, and looking eagerly at it for a little, he called to James Ainsley, our next neighbor, who was sitting at the door: "A man, Jamie, there has been an awful battle."

Jamie at once got up and drew near, and then there was a reading of the great Battle in detail and that Bonaparte had fled and was taken prisoner.

I felt a considerable interest in the relations of this battle, and especially the great loss of life, which gave me an awful horror of war and a great aversion again[st] a Red Coat and a Soldier.

The result of the Battle of Waterloo was anything but favorable to the common people, but on the contrary, it gave a new lease of power to Monarchy and Aristocracy. The iniquitous Corn Laws came out of it, subjecting the various working classes to a great deal of poverty and distress, and all the more so, as a heavy taxation was laid upon all the necessities and comforts of life.

At the May Term of 1816, my father made another change to the Farm of Ladyrig in the Parish of Roxburg[h], about two miles from Kelso. This being a very large farm, he had to keep a boy or young lad all the year around. Of course his wages were higher on this account. Having two cows with several more sheep and a certain sum of money as compensation, I therefore filled that situation, and took an active part in all the various duties of a Shepherd, thus not only supporting myself, but doing something to help and bring up the younger members of the family in a more comfortable way.

* * *

There are certain seasons of the year, when a shepherd has some special work to perform. One of these is the sheep washing and shearing. This brought us out of the ordinary routine of business into active relation with certain other parties on the farm. The washing was done in the river Teviot, which bounded the north part of the farm. To wash by hand, 30 or 40 score sheep required the help of all the servants on the place. A suitable place was chosen on the riverbank and movable hurdles were so placed, as to enclose two or three score sheep. Then a sort of division of labor was entered into. There were first five or six men standing in a line in the water, not less than three feet deep. My father, who was at the head of this work to see to it that the work was done properly, stood farthest in. The first movement took place on the bank, where certain parties caught a sheep and handed it to the first man in the water. It was thrown on its back and swayed from side to side for a little, and then handed to his next neighbor, and so on through all the parties to the end, when it was turned around on its belly, with its head to the shore, where it soon swam out. As this standing in the water for three or four hours was considered as rather a cold business, it was invariably the custom for the farmer to supply all the parties in the work with plenty of Whiskey; care, however, had to be taken not to give too much, 'til the work was done. And then it was quite a common thing to see both men and women, and I may say, also boys, going staggering home in such a way that they could scarcely walk.

It was at one of these washings that I had the first sensation of what it was to be drunk. I had occasion to drive some of the sheep from the washing back to their pasture, and in doing this, once or twice I stumbled and fell. I looked to see if any person saw me, and really felt ashamed of myself. I then formed a resolution that for the future I would always drink in moderation and not become a fool before the world. I had at that time never heard of total abstinence, and like many others, considered Whiskey as one of the creatures of God.

The next event in my shepherd life was the sheep shearing. This was generally done by the neighboring shepherding, assisting each other, and also by engaging certain parties who made sheep shearing a special business as the season came around. I commenced shearing the second year we came to this farm, and some of the strong sheep I found at first a little hard to hold and manage. However, I felt encouraged by the countenance of the old farmer whose name was Andrew Robertson. He directed me how to hold the sheep and also how to apply the shears, and by thus taking a pride in this matter, I soon attained to that perfection that very few could compete with me, and thus verified the old adage: "That they who learn young learn fair."

Another even[t] in my shepherd life was the Lambing Season. And here I may mention that all the sheep on this farm were of the long wool, pure Leicester breed. These, it is well known, are more tender and require more attention and shelter in the Lambing season than certain others. It was the practice on this farm at that season to bring the ewes who were kept warm and sheltered, and where they could be waited on at all hours by the shepherd. Here, he could go out at any hour with his lantern and attend to any that might require his help and skill. We were allowed to have our headquarters in the farm kitchen, where we kept a fire and made ourselves comfortable as circumstances would permit. This season lasted a month or more, and I took my turn every alternate night with my father. Some of these nights we were kept very busy having it out and in every hour. In this way I could sleep for a few minutes and then go out on duty and come in again and sleep. I think this gave me a sort of habit in after life, for I can take a short nap either through the day or the night and wake up and feel refreshed. This I know is not generally the case.

On the high grounds of this farm near to the Bowmont Forest, were a good deal of young plantation and the cover for game. These were protected, as they are still, with very strict laws. I had received instruction from some of the neighboring shepherds as to the best methods of snaring hares in a wire gin. I had here a fine opportunity for carrying out this business. As when looking after the sheep I could also have my eye on the place where a hare had a regular run, and where a small wire noose properly adjusted would either hang the hare or hold it a prisoner 'til I came to relieve it. The great thing in this business was to do it without being seen or suspected, for should any of the gamekeepers see me or the farmer or any of his sons, not only would I be liable to a heavy fine and imprisonment, but my father would have lost his situation at the first term.

I may mention that the proper season to catch and entrap this game was in the fall and winter half year, as only then it had a market value.

Now while attending the sheep through the day, I generally had all the places looked out to set the snares in the evening, when "Twilight grey had in her sober livery all things clad." It was indispensable that I should be up early to attend the sheep, but more especially to have my eye upon the snares. If any hares were caught they were at once concealed and all snares were removed and hid away. One necessary appendage to a shepherd was his plaid. These were made with nook or corner which formed a sort of a bag. In this, two or three hares at the left elbow could be covered with the other part of the plaid as nothing could be seen below. In this way I came home to breakfast, but with caution, lest any stranger should be in the house. I sometimes caught rabbits and partridges, but hares were the most valuable. These I readily sold for eighteen pence each or three shillings, and they were ultimately disposed of at the Edinburgh market. This was done through the village [by the cadger] Richardson, who carried on this business in a systematic way. One of the sons, whose name was Tom, came regularly round with cart through our district every Saturday. He gathered eggs and had at the same time a supply of salt, soap, sugar, snuff, and tobacco. The father went into Edinburgh every week with his large cart with the products his sons had collected, and then bringing back with him the various things for their country customers.

The house in which we lived stood by itself nearly half a mile from the farm, being all the better for doing business in a secret way. As Tom Richardson came around, he left his cart at the roadside and came into the house with an empty basket and a large sacken bag over his arm. Then he asked my mother what eggs she had, and what other things she might be wanting. If no stranger was in the house, there was another question—had she anything for the bag today? This was understood if there were any hares, and it was seldom, but there were some—sometimes as many as three or four. This, with the eggs, supplied the family with groceries and other things and also a little extra change. I had thus no compunction of conscience in violating the game laws, which are only a relic of aristocratic ascendancy, and will no doubt be modified when the working classes are endowed with their rights of political power.

After the Battle of Waterloo, when the Corn Laws and other unjust edicts were taking effect, there was a time of great distress and dissatisfaction among the manufacturing and working classes. There were some great meetings in which there was rioting and radical expression, which was at once put down by calling out the military forces. Even the newspapers of that time had to use great caution, as there were certain laws existing which made it a heavy fine with imprisonment for the writing or printing, and even the possession of certain books of a political character. I can well recollect of getting a loan of Paine's *Rights of Man*, and I got great caution not to show it, but to read it on the sly.

It was about this time in 1818 that the *Edinburgh Weekly Scotsman* first came out. It was a Liberal Whig and showed the old tricks of Tor[yism], and especially that a British subject had certain rights and that taxation and representation should go together.

When my father first heard of this paper, he had great desire to become a reader. But then the price was far beyond his reach. At that time there was a heavy tax on paper, with stamps on all newspapers ... the price of the paper was nine pence. It really seemed that the ruling powers at that time were determined to keep the great mass of people poor and ignorant. But where there is a will, there is a way, and my father devised a plan to get the paper both for himself and others. At the farm, there were eight plowmen and a steward, who lived in a range of cottage houses. Altogether he found that if each of these would pay a penny a week, he would write and procure the paper. This they consented to do, and so it came by post to the village of Heiton, where some of our family attending school brought it home in the evening. The plan for reading it the first night was for all the parties to meet at one of their houses, have all the principle news read and discussed and then every one to have it a night for themselves afterwards.

... I well recollect what a great pleasure it was for me to go down with my father and have the paper read. I was generally the reader under my father's supervision. Some of these plowmen were not much skilled in either politics or literature, and the old man, having seen and known something of the world, was in the way of making certain explanation, which made the reading much more interesting and profitable.

We had good reason to believe that our time and money was well spent and that what we were doing was an example to others. For example, there was an old acquaintance of my father, a Thomas Laidlaw, who had a sort of intellectual twist of mind, but being what was called a "spademan" or "day laborer" and having a large family was in poor circumstances, but being a reader and a keen political observer, he thought he would try the same plan as my father had done to procure the reading of the *Scotsman*. The farm on which he lived was that of Kersknow, in the parish of Eckford, and was tended by a great farmer by the name of Walker. He talked about the paper, submitted his plan and got it in the same way as my father. But a circumstance here transpired which shows how the working classes were subjected to the will of their employers at the time. The great Walker had heard that his servants were reading such a paper, and so when the first of March came around, at the time when the yearly engagements were made, the Steward got instructions to say that all who had been reading the *Scotsman* Newspaper must either give it up or otherwise they could not be engaged for another year. That, of course, ended the matter and the paper was given up.

2

Working Life and Marriage

THESE were hard times for the working classes. There was a superabundance of laborers at that time, much more than could find employment, and of course, wages were very low. The highest wage for a Spad[e]man or day laborer was 18 pence per day. Women's wages for outdoor farmwork: 10 pence or a penny an hour. This state of things continued until new fields or emigration was opened up and greater facilities for travel both by land and sea.

My father had a great wish to go out to America again, but could not for the time, as he had lent all his money (about 80 pounds) to certain parties who could not pay up at that time, but promised to pay. So, he continued as a shepherd on the farm of Ladyrig with my assistance, for the space of five years.

I can well recollect about that time that a great many people who had a thought of going out to America, used to call and consult with my father about their passage and how best to get up through the country after landing. He was thus enabled to give good information, not only from having been there himself, but from books of geography with maps, which he used to trace from New York up the Hudson to Albany and then up the Hudson or Mohawk Valley, and up the Gennesse [New York], the great wheat region in York State, and soon to the Great Lakes.

Some parties were going south to the state of Ohio, the way which was also pointed out on the map. At that time, there was another thing, which was greatly talked about as the greatest improvement ever made in the country—the Great Erie Canal.

4. View of the river Teviot at Ormiston that bounded the north
of Ladyrig farm where George Taylor spent some of his childhood.
SOURCE: MARGARET AND PETER JEARY

Its whole course was traced out to its connection with Lake Erie
and then its farther connection with the great state of Ohio and
then with the river of that name, and then with the great Mississippi to the sea. Altogether, a future prospect great and grand,
such were some of the flattering prospects held out before the
emigrants at that time. But what a change has come over, not
only in the United States, but all over the world since that day.
The power of steam, both by land and sea, with accompanying
electric service and the telegraph, has revolutionized the world.
The ends of the earth have been brought together and we see
knowledge is being multiplied abundantly.

My father left the farm of Ladyrig in 1821 and engaged as
shepherd at the Wooden, a farm in the parish of Eckford.

I was now free to work at my own hand, as is the common
Scotch phrase, with those who have no direct engagement. For
three-fourths of a year, I found in spadework and harvest on this

45

and one of the adjoining farms. My wages were 18 pence per day, except the harvest month, which was 12 shillings per week with victuals.

In the course of the summer, I got acquainted with a man by the name of Robert Renwick, who had a market garden of his own and at the same time wrought some of the farmer's gardens in the neighborhood. He was a man of intelligence, had read a good deal, and had seen and known something of the world. He had more garden work than he could rightly accomplish, so I made an engagement to work with him in the spring of 1822. In this way we wrought together for the space of eight years in the most pleasant and agreeable manner. Our wages were 18 pence per day with victuals and board. As we had often a week or more of that work in the season for which we had extra pay, and I generally took a month of harvest work which was then all done with the sickle, having the usual fare of oatmeal porridge and milk, morning and evening, with a loaf of wheat bread and a quart of beer for dinner. It was often hard work for both young and old, but a very independent life for those who could do their darg.

There was another thing, which I learned from Robert Renwick, and that was cutting and trimming hedges. Many of the gardens, being partly enclosed by a wall for growing fine fruit and the remainder by a beech hedge, which was trimmed once or twice a year. This work is all done with the hedge knife. There is a certain art and skill in handling it, so as to make it cut easily. I recollect that Renwick put me through the whole order of the work. First by keeping a loose elbow joint, while the knife is held firmly, then striking at a certain angle, as to make a clean cut. There are knives of all dimensions. Some are light and a little hook shaped for cutting the one-year sprays, and some are strong and heavy for cutting down an old hedge with stems as thick as your arm. We had often a job of this kind in winter, when we could not dig and do garden work, by contracting with the farmers to do this work or to dress the hedges for miles along each side of the public roads. In this gardening and hedgework, both Renwick and myself found a sort of independence, as we could have a day or a week or more at any time for our own pleasure.

I think it was in the end of 1822 and the beginning of 1823 that I first visited the city of Edinburgh. That city had been honored with a visit from his Royal Highness, George IV. This last year the new buildings, especially in the "New Town" were at that time going on with a great boom. It so happened that Mrs. Renwick had a sister married in Edinburgh, who was sometimes in the way of visiting her friends in the country in summer while they in turn, made a reciprocal visit in winter.

Robert Renwick proposed that if I would make a visit to Edinburgh with him, it would cost me no more than traveling expenses. This I concluded to do, and so we started from Kelso, with the stagecoach at 8 o'clock in the morning. I had never been out of the country of Roxburgh before and therefore I started with high prospects. The fare, I think, was altogether ten shillings, eight-coach fare, and the other for the guard and driver. This was outside fare on the top of the coach, which to me was greatly preferable, as from this I could much better see the various places and the country as we passed along. We went by the way of Smailholm and changed horses at Earlston. Then up the Leader Water to Lauder and on to Carf[r]ae Mill, where there was an Inn and another change of horses. This stage was considered about half way to the city, from this two miles up the glen and then we were at the foot of Soutra Hill. Then the winding up and round about this hill took some little time. But after getting up and along the ridge for a mile, we came to an Inn with stabling called Louries Den, and I well recollect of seeing a large board placed against the side of the house with the motto of invitation, "Come taste of the Porter, you'll find the road a great deal shorter."[3]

We now descended the hill and passed several other places of note, till we came to the old town of Dalkeith, and then along the throng-road of 7 miles to Edinburgh. When we came into the city things seemed to look awful big to me. The oil lamps

47

were just being lighted (gas having not yet been introduced). This with the coal smoke hanging over gave me the first introduction to Auld Reekie.

The coach stopped at High Street on the east corner of North Bridge. There were a great many men, they called porters with ropes and straps round their shoulders to carry any trunk or other baggage, which passengers might have, to their destination. Mr. Renwick engaged one to carry his trunk to No. 2 Northumberland, in the New Town. We walked after him, and this was my first view of what then was to me the Great City.

After seeing the friends and having refreshments for an hour or two, one of the party, a young man, proposed to take [me] out and show me some of the principle parts of the city by lamp light. It was all strange to me, but I recollect we crossed Princes Street, passed up what was called the Mound, which was then only a narrow Strip of what it is now. And I recollect, up near the top, a little below where the Free Church Assembly Hall now stands, there were some Shows, and my friend and guide gave me a treat to go in and see the performances of one of them. After some Sleigh[t]-hand tricks were gone through, and some other thing—a Learned Pig was introduced which could spell out certain words that were required by selecting from an Alphabet of Cards, which were lying promiscuous, those in their order that made the perfect word.

We then went up and down High Street, where among many others, were a great many Soldiers going up and down from the Castle. And here I met with a little surprise which was a Soldier walking with two young Ladies, with whom I got acquainted the last year in the Harvest Field: this was at the Farm of Court Hill, about three miles from Kelso. The Soldier urged me to take one of the girls, but I knew that they bore the character of what is called Free and Easy, and so I suppose they were carrying out their So[i]ree in the big City.

In going down High Street, my guide showed me some of the big things and also some of the little bad things. These last were a certain Class of young women standing about the head of W[y]nds on each side of the Street, and if you looked at them, would at once put the question, "Ar e guan te take is wie the night?" I have often met them in other parts of the City looking for their game.

Our visit lasted for about ten days, so that in that time I had a good opportunity of seeing the many great sights of the City and its surroundings.

In May 1822, my Father had removed to Crailing Tofts as Shepherd, where he remained four years. I was always at home on the Saturday Evening, and a regular attendant at the Presbyterian Church at Jedburgh on the Sabbath. I was admitted to that Church the same year as a member under the ministry of the Reverend Peter Young. It was a large Church and Congregation, having been built in 1818.

There was another large Church built the same year called the Relief, then under the Ministry of the Reverend James Porteous. There were two great times then with these Churches each year. These were the winter and Summer Sacraments. On this occasion, the first service commenced on Thursday, which was called the Fast Day, when Two Sermons were preached. Then on Saturday at one o' clock were religious exercises with a Sermon and a distribution of Token[s] by the Minister under the watchful eyes of the Session for admission to the Lord's Table on the Sabbath. Then on that day of Service commenced at 10 o'clock with Praise and Prayer, and then what was called the Action Sermon was preached by the Minister. He would have two or three other[s] assisting him in the remaining Services. The next thing in order was what was called the Fencing of the Tables. This was to show who were worthy Communicants and who were not. This was [done] by one of the assistants. The number of Table Services were five or six. A few special seats only being set apart for that purpose.

The first Table Service commenced with those who were already seated and were addressed for some time by one of the

49

Ministers. Then the distribution of the Bread with certain appropriate words and then that of the Cup in much the same way. As the Table was dismissed and the people passed out, and as they were being filled by another Company, the Precentor gave out the line of a Psalm, started to the Tune of Coleshill, and continued with all the Congregation singing till the Table was again filled, and then the same service was gone through with another of the Ministers. It was well through the afternoon before all these Services came to a conclusion. And then one of the Ministers gave what was called the Direction to all the members, as to how they should conduct themselves, when they should go out into the World. The conclusion for the day was a Sermon called the Evening Exercises. It was generally about half past six or seven before all was got through. It was a long day together, and more laborious to some in the Country who had seven or eight miles to walk home. The whole of this Sacramental Occasion was concluded on the Monday by the Preaching of two more Sermons.

It seems to me, as I look back at these things, that there was far too much labor and ceremony, not quite [in] harmony with the simplicity of the Omnipotence and the living truth of the Gospel.

I was always fond of Books, and at that time Sir Walter Scott and Byron were the most popular. I sometimes got a reading of such as these at some [of] the Gentlemen's Houses, where I was working Gardens. It was also about this time that I got a share in what was called Balfours Library in Jedburgh. This I purchased from my sister Mary's Husband, Robert Stevenson, who was about to leave for Edinburgh. It had many of the Standard authors, including the Encyclopedia Britannica.

It was in the beginning of 1826 that my Father gave up his situation, intending to go to America. I can recollect that in April I went to Hawick to see a Ship Agent there of the name of Gentle and found out all about the rate of passage. But some of our best laid plans 'gang aft agley,' and so went this, for the money that my father had loaned could not be made available. And so our voyage was given up and Cot House or a dwelling without engagement was taken in the Village of Eckford. My Father took work in the time of haying and harvest and I kept on in my gardening operations.

I recollect that the summer of 1826 was one the most remarkable for drought and an early Harvest of any that was ever known in that Country. What I recollect about the early Harvest was that I was at St. Boswells Fair on the 16th of July, and commenced my regular Harvest on the day following. The Wheat Crop was extra fine but Oats and Barley were short. The 26th of May, the Flitting day was a thorough wet out and out, but there was not another drop for three months.

I recollect that in our church relations, the Rev. Peter Young died in the end of 1824. The Reverend William Nicol was subsequently called and ordained in September 1826. He was a popular preacher and the large church was crowded every Sabbath. I was a regular attendant on his ministry for eighteen years and would walk over 10 miles every Sabbath.

I think I made my second visit to Edinburgh in the winter of 1827. This time I thought I would walk the journey and save the ten shillings for coach, and spend the money on books. I therefore started from Eckford on a moonlit morning about two o'clock. I went by the way of Smailholm, Earlston, and Lauder, and on to Carfrae Mill. I had studied before what to eat and drink by the way, so I put a cake of gingerbread in my pocket to eat that at different times. I took a drink when thirsty, of clear spring water by the way, and so when I came to Louries Den on the top of Soutra, I did not taste of the porter but kept walking on down the hill and on to Dalkeith and so on, till I arrived at the Old City about 4 o'clock. I had thus walked that altogether nearly fifty miles. The only thing I felt was my feet a little bluish, it being somewhat frosty and the road hard.

After having tea and refreshment at my sister's house, then on Brown Street, I went across to the New Town, and made some calls on parties whom I knew. They were much surprised and could scarcely believe that I had come from home that morning. One of my great resorts, while in the city, was hunting through the book store and attending some of their cheap sales. In this way, I sometimes got some great bargains, but often spent a good deal more than what I saved from the coach hire.

When the weather was [so] frosty that I could not do garden work, I have sometimes stayed a month in the city, and by this means I got well acquainted with its various institutions. I generally came home the same way on foot, so that my travelling and board cost me a very little.

My father made an engagement at the term of 1827 to be again the Shepherd at Wooden. My brothers, Alexander and James were hired out to farm service. My father, not being very stout, I often used to assist him in the Lambing season, especially at night. As it was imperative at that time for all householders on a farm to furnish an outworker, my sister Agnes, supplied that want for several years. And as a proof that she was strong and healthy, she proposed one winter to walk with me and see Edinburgh. I said that it could not be expected that she could walk all the way, but if we started early in the morning about two o'clock and walk so far on the way, then take the coach when it came up with us. So we started and she walked well, often going ahead of me, and we were a good deal more than half way when the coach came up with us. But here our plan went aglee, for it so happened that day the coach was loaded to the full— so much, that they could not take on another passenger.

"Well then," I said, "We will take lodgings by the way when you tire." And so she kept on going ahead and sometimes slyly hinting that I was getting tired and to come on. In this way, she kept on going ahead, and we arrived at sister Mary's house in Edinburgh about four o'clock.

After tea and refreshment, we went out and made a call on some of our Southern friends, and it was very hard to make them believe that we had come from home that morning. I have never

5. Wester Wooden farm, Eckford, where George Taylor's father and brother James both worked as shepherd at different times.
SOURCE: MARGARET AND PETER JEARY

heard of any of our American Ladies that could make such a walk as this.

In 1829 my father's health began to fail. For a good many years his stomach was in a bad condition, and was often subject to what was called the waterbrash. He had now frequent fits of coughing and his appetite began to fail. For sometime previous he was fully aware that he was dying, gave charge to me to look after my mother and the youngest members of the family, and even about how his funeral should be conducted. On the Saturday evening he was speaking earnestly with my mother, when he desired me also to come to the bedside, saying his time was now drawing near. I had earnest prayer with him, in which he seemed very happy. My mother also was quite calm and resigned. He passed rather a restless night, and in the morning his face gave signs that death was near. About 8 o'clock, after a slight spasm, he breathed his last. This was on the 9th of August, 1829. His age was only sixty years.

53

It was the custom then, in Scotland to write letters of invitation to all parties, whom we wished to attend the funeral. And this took me a good deal of labor. Another custom was then prevalent of giving a service of a glass of wine or whiskey followed with shortbread cake all round the company. As I thought there was no use in this I wished to let it lye over but my mother wished it otherwise, as she said the folk would speak about us.

The funeral took place on the 19th at Eckford Churchyard. There were no women who went in the funeral procession to the graveyard, only men. All the company stood around the grave till the Sexton filled in the clay and laid on the turf. And then the friend at the head, when all was finished would say, "My friends, I am very much obliged for your attendance at this time".

My brother James had been taking charge of the sheep for the last few months, whilst I occasionally gave him help and advice. And some of the neighbor shepherds were also very friendly. I was always at home on Saturday evening and Sundays.

I recollect about the end of the year 1829, this was the occasion of the birth of Andrew Stevenson. (My sister Mary's only son). My mother made a visit to Edinburgh and stopped a few weeks. My sister Agnes keeping the house at home. I think it was the year following [or 1833] that she was married to William Huggan, Millwright, at Jedburgh.

It was about this time that there was a good deal of agitation all over the nation, both politics and religion. George IV died in 1830 and was succeeded by his brother William IV. The Catholic Relief Bill had given some fear to the State Church for the safety of Protestantism. And now an urgent demand had arisen for a more full and equal representation of the people in Parliament. This brought on the great agitation for the Reform Bill of 1832. The two great parties were Whigs and Tories and a few Radicals, these last held that Taxation without Representation was Despotism. This was all the more glaring from the place and relation of what was called the Rotten Boroughs in England, the most [of] which were only represented by one or two individuals, some of which had their seat in the House of Lords.

In Scotland at that time, things were only a little comparatively better. As an instance of this, a little previous to the passing of the bill, a member for the County of Roxb[u]rghshire had to be elected, occasioned by the death of its member, Sir Alex. Don. This election took place in the Town Hall of Jedburgh. I succeeded after a scramble in getting a seat in the gallery and looking down on the privileged voters below. The whole number being only 150. This number for a county of fifty thousand. The candidates were Sir William Elliot of Stobbs, Whig and honorable Henry Scot[t] Merton, Tory. Among these privileged few sat the great Sir Walter Scott. I had never seen him before: he sat very dull and sleepy-like. The clerk had a list of the voters, and as he read out their names, each one answered by naming their candidates. I heard Sir Walter vote for Mr. Scott when called, and Mr. Scott was elected by a majority. I [had] a list of those 150 voters in a Kelso Per[iodical] of 1884, and it stated that only one of that number was alive today.

The agitation that was going all over the country while this was pending was very great and made a far greater demand for newspapers. I know this was so with myself. They were neither so plentiful no[r] so cheap as they are now, but I recollect I was so fortunate as to get a reading of the *London Daily Times* for two years. It rather came to me in a round about way. In the first place, two young men in London got it, then it was sent by mail coach to their father in Kelso. Then he sent it by post to his friend Mr. Lillie, Crailing, and then I got it from him at the price of one penny per paper. By this means I got posted up with all the doings in Parliament and all the great meetings that were being held through the nation.

It gave an opportunity for men of talent to come to the front, such as Joseph Hume for Scotland, Brougham for England, and O'Connell for Ireland. Earl Grey and Lord John Russell had the honor to carry it through both houses of Parliament. This Reform

Bill was only the beginning of Reforms, and some of these are being carried out in a higher scale. ... One great reason for this political war was that the Church's one petition [had] entirely ignored all [that] the Dissenting Churches had done and was doing in building Churches and teaching the people. The Church Petition was in the hands and management of the Minister of the Parish, the Rev. Joseph Yair (who is still living). He got a day ahead of me and was very urgent for signatures. One reason I was told, which he especially gave, was that it was to obtain the Gospel free to all without money and without price. I succeeded in getting a majority of the names in the Parish.

One great thing against the State Church was the Law of Patronage, which was in the hand of one man to present a minister to the people of the Church and Parish when vacancy occurred. Not only was this held up as a glaring evil against the Church by Dissenters, but Dr. Chalmers and his party also found it to be the only great stumbling which stood in their way of reformation. In order to meet and overcome this the Evangelical Party passed what they called the Veto Law, by which it was declared: "That it is a fundamental law of this Church that no Pastor shall be introduced in any congregation contrary to the will of the people, and so enacted that a solemn dissent of a majority of male heads of families' members of the vacant congregation and in full communion with the Church shall be deemed sufficient ground for the rejection of the precentor." This veto act was soon the subject of litigation in the Court of Session. A verdict affirmed by the House of Lords was to the effect: "That the rejection of the presenter on the ground of this dissent was illegal and that the civil courts had a right to review and control all proceedings of Church Courts."

As the law was thus decided the majority with Dr. Chalmers came to the conclusion that they could no longer remain consistently with the Established Church of Scotland. This great contest was brought to a termination at the meeting of the General Assembly on the 18th of May, 1843. Four hundred and seventy four ministers led the way of an immense crowd. There was one plan which Dr. Chalmers had devised, and is peculiar to the Free Church, called the Sustentation Fund.

My brother James continued as shepherd at [Wooden] till the Term of 1832 when John Park, the Master, had a favorite; he wished to occupy his place. This broke up our family arrangement as a home. In a family consultation we thought if he could find another place as shepherd it might be best for the present. We therefore attended the Hiring Markets of Kelso and Jedburgh, but no situation turned up. We then took a Cot House at Ormiston. My mother was working on the farm and James found some spade work in the neighborhood. I had got my brother apprenticed a year before to a country tailor, so that they were often all at home on Saturday night and Sunday.

My youngest sister, Margaret, had gone to service with the Lady at Wrens Nest, Jedburgh, and my youngest brother John, was at school.[4] When spring came round James thought he would like to go to America, but had not quite sufficient money. I said I would remove that objection by giving him what was needful. And so he resolved to go. We gave him a large chest to hold his clothes and provisions, the very chest that my father and mother took thirty years before and brought back again. This same old chest is still at Delhi [Michigan] with our friends, the Mables. I saw it at that place in 1875.

James therefore left us in the spring of 1833, had about a month['s] passage, and arrived at New York, and from there on to Delhi, where he stopped a few weeks with our cousins. He then left for Caledonia in New York State where he was hired and got good wages. But the great boom for the west came and so he started out and came to Kalamazoo or Bronson in the end of 1835.

About the beginning of 1835 I made an engagement with Mr. William Mein of Ormiston to work and take care of his garden and grounds, but in doing this I made the bargain, so as to preserve my independence. I was to [have] a free house, all the potatoes I might require, and a certain amount of money. I could engage other men to help do the work. And then I was at liberty to go and work at other places. There was one great advantage in this, that my mother could do a great deal of the work in hoeing and weeding, taking the fruits and vegetables to the house, and being about on the place in my absence. Her services gave a great satisfaction to the servants and the Lady of the house. In this engagement I was induced to do a great deal of h[a]rd work. There was a great deal of lawn grass to mow and in doing this I often used to rise at three or four o'clock in the morning, and then walk two or three miles to do a day's work at another garden.

In this way I was enabled to make some extra money, but I had to work well for it. After my brother Andrew had served his apprenticeship he though[t] he would like to go South and follow out his business. So with some aid from me he went to Manchester in England and found work there for over a year in some of the best houses. This made him complete in business. After hearing encouraging news from James, he thought he also would like to go to America, but for this he had not sufficient money. Here again I advanced him the necessary amount, and my mother also got him a good outfit of all the necessary provisions. I mentioned that if my life was spared, it was my intention to come out to America, but in the mean time, I would entrust him with the sum of twenty pounds or a hundred dollars, to be laid out on land, either by himself or brother James, for me, suitable for garden or nursery purposes, and therefore I wrote out the following note to which he affixed his signature and from which I here copy:

"I do hereby affix my signature to show that I received the sum of 20 pounds from George Taylor, my brother, to be delivered to his brother James in America or otherwise to be appropriated for his benefit by either of us as witness my hand, this 18th day of April 1836. Signed Andrew Taylor."

He thus left with some other young men of his acquaintance, also going out to try their fortune. They arrived in New York in about a month of the usual sea voyage. I believe he wrought for a few months in New York or some other of the eastern cities. But in corresponding with his brother James he was induced to come west to Kalamazoo, and there commenced the business of tailor and clothier.

The winter of 1836 and that of 1837 was remarkable for a long and severe frost. There was comparatively little snow on the low grounds. All the rivers and lakes were frozen and skating was a great amusement with certain parties. I well remember a circumstance that occurred in this connection on the river Teviot at Kale Waterfoot. For about ¾ of a mile above the Ormiston Mill Caul, the water formed a pool or a lake, and there were certain young men in the neighborhood who were in the way of meeting and skating all over this piece of water. A slight thaw had occurred, which caused a melting of the snow on the hills, and by this, the Kale Water had been brought down in such a way as to break up a small portion of the ice at its mouth. But shortly after a sharp frost had again set in freezing it over, and then this was followed by a slight fall of snow. There were one of these young men who had been in the way of skating on this place, a James Ord of [Upper Nisbet]. In coming home from the Kelso Market, instead of going around a little by the Chain Bridge, he went straight through across the Teviot on the ice where he had been previously skating, but he not being aware that a portion of this ice had recently been broke up and the snow covering it the same as the other. It gave away with him and after a struggle, as was apparent from the broken ice, his body was carried downstream. Not coming on the Friday evening as expected, search was made. At about 12 o'clock the Steward at [Nisbet] called at my house telling what they supposed had happened. They took our boat to aid them in finding the body. We lifted the boat into a long cart and went to the place. We had axes and saws. Our plan was to cut a certain breadth downward, the boat being placed across in the water and a man at each end with a long drawn hook of 10 or 12 feet

6. Kalemouth Chain Bridge, over the river Teviot.
This bridge carries a public road across the Teviot,
just above the mouth of the Kale water.
SOURCE: MARGARET AND PETER JEARY

long (this being the depth of the water). I took one end of the boat, raking [the] bottom of the lake with the long hook. There was a keen frost and I found my hands far colder under water than out. But we were bountifully supplied with Whiskey, which deadened the feeling of cold for the time. We worked unsuccessfully all night. It was decided that the body was carried down to the Caul, 200 yards below. I agreed to begin working there, but first I desired them to draw the boat back a little so I might make two or three last throws below ice. I made one throw and nothing, but at the next one I found the hook had caught something. I held on and called for the other party to put down their hooks near to mine. We both pulled gently, then appeared the head of the body with its yellow hair.

It was most singular and fortunate that I found it at the very last, for otherwise had we begun the next morning at the Caul and wrought upward it would have been two days or more before we would have wrought up to the place where the body was found. It was at once put into the cart among straw and covered with a cloth.

I at once turned my face for home, having about ½ mile to walk. As my clothes were wet I was nearly stiff frozen before I got there. It was with some difficulty that my clothes could be taken off, and then I found I had got a good many cuts and bruises on my hands and arms. These I had not felt by reason of the cold, the excitement, and the whiskey; but I felt the effects of them for days and weeks afterwards.

I now return to relate something of my own personal history where I had my home with my mother at Ormiston. I had never yet seen it proper to enter into a marriage relation, though I had many opportunities presented at the various places where I was working the gardens. I know I had great attention paid me by many of the servant girls, some of which were good looking and attractive, but as I always looked upon this relation from a Christian position, I was somewhat cautious in entering upon it. After coming to Ormiston I got acquainted with one of the servant maids of the Gentleman's House. Her name was Helen Robson and was of a respectable family in the neighborhood. She was a church member and I had good reason to think from our conversation on religious subjects that she was truly what she professed to be. Our marriage was fixed on the 19th of January, 1837. We arranged to make a trip to Edinburgh, and so early in the morning of that day, we were united at the Presbyterian Manse in Kelso by the Reverend Henry Benton.

We then had breakfast and took the stagecoach at 9 o'clock for Edinburgh, where we arrived betwixt three and four in the afternoon. We went to my sister Mary's house, and were well entertained. And then she had a room and private lodgings engaged for us from a Mr. Horn at No. 1 Richmond Place. We spent about 14 days in and around the city, seeing many of the great things and calling upon some of our old acquaintances.

We also had a trip up the Firth of Forth by Steamer to Stirling. I had never been there before, and so I had great pleasure on viewing the fine scenery on each side. We spent two days viewing the Old City and its surroundings, and then came back in the [same] way to Edinburgh.

We did not commence our housekeeping till the 26th of May, and this was in a house in the same connection with that which my mother occupied. As the place and the people were all familiar, my wife seemed to be very happy in her new situation, and her relations with my mother were in every way agreeable.

Our first trial of affliction occurred about the end of October. In her very hard labor in giving birth to a strong healthy man child, and which in the language of a great poet, "was strangled in life's porch".[5]

She was very ill for some time. But being of a good constitution, she ultimately got over it and enjoyed good health. All things went only agreeable with us till sometime in the month of May 1839. She spent some weeks in a very painful feeling, and about the 24th under great distress gave birth to a still born child, and from which she died the following day.

She was buried in Eckford Churchyard along side of where my father was in 1829. This was a very distressing circumstance to both myself and her friends, but these things after a little time close up again, and the more so when we are actively engaged in our worldly callings.

I had previously entered as a member in both the Horticultural Societies of Kelso and Jedburgh. And about that time there had arose quite a strong feeling of competition in both fruits and flowers. The culture of the Dahlia merely as a showy single flower was introduced about 1826. In every year they had been improving that flower by cross impregnation till now it was become a round double ball. Some new and improved varieties were coming out every year, and that such had received the Gold Medal last year at the Royal Horticultural Society. The price of such were advertised to be sent out in spring at ten shillings and

7. Springwood Park, Kelso, where George Taylor
planted many trees that remain to this day.
SOURCE: MARGARET AND PETER JEARY

six pence each. These had all names according to their charac-
teristics. A delicate tinted white would be the Princess Victoria,
a bright crimson would be Cardinal Perretti, and some other
bold color, the Duke of Wellington. Great prizes were thus given
by our Societies in competition for these, often a prize of 10 or
20 shillings for a single bloom of one of these last years' varieties.
The prize for the best 6 and the best 12 varieties, and sometimes
what they called a sweepstakes for the best 12 or 24, each
competitor paying in 5 or 10 shillings, and the best took the
whole amount.

The garden at Ormiston was walled round with all the finest
fruit trees trained in both the fan and horizontal manner. They
were in a fine bearing state and I often carried off some of the
best prizes, and this was all the more honorable as I had some
strong parties to compete against at Kelso. I had the gardeners
of the [Duke] of Roxburgh, Newton Don,[6] [Mitchell?], [Hender-
syde] Park, Pinnacle Hill, and Springwood Park, and many others.
At Jedburgh, I had to compete with Bonjedward, Monteviot,
Ancrum, [Chesters], and Minto in Jedwater.

But in the competition for the Dahlia Prizes, I was especially successful; sometimes sweeping the whole board and carrying off more than 5 pounds. For these alon[e] I had a piece of the best land for growing them, and they had my best personal attention.

My youngest brother John, in some way got his arm hurt while a small boy. I kept him at school in order that he might make a living without hard work. He tried school teaching, but as he had no inclination for it, and as his arm had gotten pretty stout, he rather was inclined to follow out gardening, and as I had to hire help to do this work, he turned in and wrought with me till 1845.

There was one thing in which I had always taken a great interest in since I came to this district, and that was fishing, and here in the Teviot and the Kale, I had a fine chance to carry it out. In the summer evenings with the Rod and Fly, and when some of the large trout came up the stream, I frequently filled a basket of very fine large ones. There was another time in the fall and winter, when the river was flooded. I often caught a great many with what was called the pouch net. This was a net in the form of a bag with a large mouth sewed to an iron frame, with a mortise in which a wooden handle of 10 or 12 feet was fixed. The place to throw this was in the eddy of a stream, where a trout or salmon might be resting, and by pulling it down stream and drawing it out, you would sometimes have the pleasure of seeing a large trout[,] and sometimes a salmon came stumbling out.

But there was a certain season of the year called 'Closetime', in which we had to use caution in doing this work. This season was sometime in November till February, and so if I had been found by some of the Water Bailiffs using such a net at this time, I would have been liable to a very heavy fine. But I must confess that I was sometimes tempted to break this law when a flood came and knowing 2 or 3 casts in the river near to my garden and house, I frequently ventured out in the dark and had a successful throw when there was no Water Bailiff to see me.

These fishing and Game Laws have in a great measure their origin and support from a landed aristocracy; and there is now every reason to suppose when the people are more fully represented that these and all such laws will either be done away with or greatly amended.[7]

* * *

My old grandmother had been stopping with my mother for sometime, being now very feeble with certain symptoms that her end was drawing near. The Rev. Joseph Yair for some time was a regular visitor and she appreciated his visits very much. And when she died he attended her funeral all the way to Ho[w]nam Kirk. Her age was nearly 95 years. She had a good memory and could tell some old interesting stories, which she had witnessed on the borders.

As I had been in the way of attending to the garden at [Grahamslaw] for some time, I there got acquainted with who was to be my second wife and the mother of my family. Her name was Jane Dodds. Her father and brother John were for a long time Blacksmiths at the village of Bonjedward. We were married there at her father's house in the month of March 1842, and I brought her direct home that same night to our house at Ormiston, which was already furnished to enter.

Her relation with my mother was most cordial and everything that could be desired. Since I had come to Ormiston as gardener, I had also been at the same time Forester taking charge of the young plantation. Mr. William Mein had bought this Estate sometime in 1820 and commenced at once to make great improvements, especially in the way of Timber planting. In the course of ten years he had planted more than 100 acres. About a quarter of this was on the higher Moorland and consisted of Scotch and Austrian Pine, Norway Spruce, and Larch. There was a broad strip bordering the Property on the West Side for nearly a mile. This was planted with the best hardwood mixed with [a] certain quantity of the pines and larch to act as nurses for a certain time. Some of those that had been first now much crowded and required the skillful hand of a Forester. The old gentleman died in 1836 and his oldest son Robert came home from about the plantations, and if I had time and understood how it should be done, he would be glad for me to undertake it. I mentioned that I had been working several winters with the Duke of [Buccleuch's] Forester and was on intimate terms with the Foresters of the Marquis of Lothian, and the Duke of Roxburgh, and that as the winter season [was] for such work, I would look out for a few proper men to go through with me. I therefore had some consultation with above Foresters and consulted some of the best books on that subject. I got a proper set of tools, consisting of axes, saws, pruning chisels—and with about half a dozen men commenced operations.

My work was principally to go before mark or blaze those trees to be cut out. When cut down and side branches are pruned off and the trees of cut wood are piled together. The great thing to be studied was to give proper head room for the hardwood and at the same time prune off any lateral branches getting too strong for the leader.

After going through one of those thick plantations for the first time, it seemed very destructive to one not acquainted with the business. The farm steward thought so and reported to Mr. Mein that I was destroying the whole woods. Mr. Mein came to me and said I was certainly overdoing the thing. I said I had been giving considerable attention to this matter both from observation and the study of the best authorities on Forestry, and it was just in this way that the work could be properly done.

"Well," he said, "Go on. I have no doubt that you are right and I am wrong." And so in this way in the course of two or three seasons the whole plantations were gone through. I thus got fully initiated into the art of forestry. And so it was when I look at our great country and see all the valuable timber being cut down, and so little comparatively done in the way of planting to meet the greater demands of the future—it is this that has prompted me to deliver several addresses before our Horticultural Society of Michigan on Hedging and Forestry.

Short time after this, Mr. Mein was induced from certain financial reason to sell this Estate to the Marquis of Lothian. It was then let as a farm to a Mr. William Broad with a condition that the garden and grounds be kept in the same conditions as they had been. I therefore agreed with him to do the work on the same conditions as I had done with Mr. Mein. The garden both on the wall and the standard trees produced a great deal of the very finest fruit, and this I sold at high prices.

* * *

The Ribston Pippin Apple here was the most superior; wherever I showed it, it took prizes. The soil being of a clay loam all the fruit was of a superior order and hence when offered for sale brought extra prices. In the time that I was there I sold as much fruit as nearly paid my wages.

3
Travel and Temperance

I SEE from a family record that my oldest daughter, Isabella, was born on the 19th of December, 1842. My mother being our next door neighbor gave her experience and attention to all our wants.

The following year, 1843, was famous for the great disruption in the Established Church, when Dr. Chalmers and his party left it and inaugurated the Free Church, of Scotland. All the ministers that came out carried the majority of their hearers, and they set about building a new church. In the meantime they secured temporary places such as barns, workshops, public halls.

As I had been opposed to them, while connected with the Establishment, now that they had come out, I entered heartily into their movements.

As an instance of this, in the adjacent parish of Crailing, the minister, a Rev. Milroy and leading members were looking around for a temporary place for preaching services on the Sabbath. One of the leaders spoke to me about it. The only suitable place I could see was a large grainery at the end of the Chain Bridge. But it belonged to a man that had no regard for religion and would not have church people near to him. However, as I knew him well I approached him gently about church matters and how this party at Crailing were in want of a place till their church was built, and how his grainery with very little trouble, could be made available for them on the Sabbath, stating also they would pay him for it. He said he did not want any payment but did not care to have such a meeting about the place. I insisted that he should grant the place and I added he would get the blessing of God. This idea he scouted but after a little he said he sympathized with them especially in the pluck they had shown in leaving the Auld Kirk, and that I could let them know they might have it. If they would send some proper person along he would help them to fix it up for their convenience. This was done and Mr. Milroy had large meetings every Sabbath till their own church was finished. I frequently worshipped with them instead of walking all the way to Jedburgh and sometimes acted as Pre[c]ent[o]r in leading their praise.

In some places the Parties of the Free Church had great difficulties in obtaining proper sites, especially from some of the great landlords who were opposed. Some were forced to give way from force of public sentiment. It seemed in many cases that the Lord wrought with them. There was one particular case of this sort of which I was told in connection with the building of the Free Church at the village of Morebattle. In their beginning to build a church in that place, among the first things they wanted was sand for mixing with lime and mortar. There was a place on the Kale Water near by called [Grubbit] Mill, where was generally a good supply of this material, but certain parties had taken it all away. Another party near by who had a good store was applied to but being opposed to the Free Church, they would not let them have it, even though offered a high price. This as I was told, took place on the Saturday, but it so happened that on that night, an unusual heavy rain fell on Cheviot Hills, which brought down the Kale in a violent flood and deposited at the eddy of the mill such a fine bed of sand which was more than sufficient for the whole building. This fact I had from the Miller at [Grubbit], who was a member of the Church.

It was in this year of 1843, sometime in the month of August that I started for an excursion on Northwest Scotland. I took the stagecoach along with my brother-in-law, William Huggan from Jedburgh. It being on the eve of Harvest, the country looked beautiful. In coming near Edinburgh, I noticed bills posted up announcing a railroad excursion on the following day to Glasgow and from thence to [Ayr] and the Land of Burns. The price for the round trip was seven shillings. I said to my friend, Huggan that I would go. He did not seem inclined at first, but thinking it over, he thought he would go. There were several things that made this trip interesting to me. It was new ground and I had never seen the city of Glasgow. Then I never had before been on a Railway Carriage. And the pleasure of seeing what I had read so much about, the Land of Burns.

The time of start was 8 o'clock and the depot was then at the west part of the city. It was an immensely long train, said to consist of over 1,500 passengers. There were some open carriages, and I preferred one of these, as by this I could obtain the best view of the country. We got started, and as the carriages began to move a little quick, my first sensation was that the wind was rising, and I expressed this to my friend Huggan, but scarcely had the word gone out of my mouth, before I saw the cause. But he got his laugh against me and told it afterwards. I enjoyed the varied scenery. As we went along in one place for two or three miles, we passed through solid walls of granite and at other places through beautiful fields of grain and turnips. Then when we came near the city, the engines were reversed and we were let slowly down a long tunnel, which landed us right into the city. Here we were instructed to walk through the streets and across the Clyde to the Station. This we did, having had a good look at some of the big things in passing. Having got into the carriages again, we kept moving on by the way of Paisley, and so on through other places till we reached [Ayr]. Here, we required some refreshments. And in the place was shown us where Tam O'Shanter and a Souter Jonnie used to enjoy themselves over their reaming swats. The Brigg O'Doon was nearly three miles distant. Here some of the more delicate took carriages, but the greater portion walked, as I did. Some of Tam O' Shanter notable places were pointed out in his famous raid, the place where the Packam was 'snoored away' the Kinaves,[8] the place where drunken Charlie broke [his] neck bone, the place also where hunter found the murdered bairn, and also where Mungo's Mither hanged herself. Passing on, we came to the house where Burns was born, and it was crowded. I noticed a very old lady who was resident there, and whom some of the genteel people were asking questions about Burns. I saw she did not seem to understand their language very well, and so I put some of their questions to her in good broad Scotch. She at once brightened up and said, "Aye a ken what e say". And we got into a talk, very much to the delight of the audience. Among other things, I asked her if she remembered when Burns first went away to visit Edinburgh.

"Aye," she said, "a mind it as weel as yesterday. An he had a dog and it waud gand wi him, and we had to take haund of is and bard up." She would have talked on with us, but we had to push on and see other things. This old lady, I learned, was the real Tam O'Shanter's wife. His real name as I learned was Tom Goudie, or in plain English, Thomas Goldie. I was the more interested in this interview, as in about six weeks after this, I saw in a newspaper an account of her death and who she was.

I went to see of the old Alloway Kirk. It was in a ruinous state. The roof pretty off and the windows out. In the churchyard I saw the grave and tombstone of Burns' father.

We then visited the River Doon and the Auld Brigg. And an arrangement was made to come to order, when "Ye Banks and Braes" was heartily sung by the whole multitude. There was sort of a museum and monument there, where we saw a great many relic[s] of the great Bard. Five hours were allowed us when we started from Ayr to visit the Doon and its surroundings. And so we returned back in time to look around the old city and see the "Twa Briggs" and certain other notable things. We then got on the railway, a little before six o'clock, came to Glasgow and walked through the city, then on to Edinburgh, where we arrived all safe about ten o'clock.

In a day or two after this, I formed a plan to see some of the most noted sights in Stirling and the west of Perthshire, being the more famous for the scenery of Sir Walter Scott's *Lady of the Lake*. For this purpose, I took the steamer, which starts from Granton, in the morning for Stirling. I had traveled this route once before, but it was winter and now the whole landscape and the various scenery were in the finest order.

Having been furnished with a guidebook, describing the places and the scenery on each side of the Forth, I therefore had chosen a situation where I sat on the stern or forefront of the vessel, with book in hand, taking notes of anything remarkable. While in this position, a young gentleman came up near me and asked if that was a guidebook I had got. I replied it was. I said that possibly I was a little more fortunate in that way than he was, as a friend of mine in the city was a bookseller, had made me a present of this. But I said, pointing to a space alongside, if it were his pleasure to sit down here, he might share the benefit along with me. He said he would be happy to do so, and took the place. He had a notebook and at once commenced to use it, and also a Sketch Book which he used for taking a view of any special object. And when we came to the Links of the Forth and some of the adjacent scenery, he seemed quite delighted, and the more so, as he was familiar with their history.

In an interval, he asked how far I intended to go, and I said that I intended to visit the lake and the surrounding scenery. "Why," he said, "that is just where I am going and I shall be most happy that we go together."

In a little time we arrived at the wharf at Stirling, and as I had been there before, I led the way up through the city. We made inquiry for the coach office and found that it did not start for Callender till 4 o'clock. We then secured our tickets for outside seats on the coach, as at this season it was crowded.

We had thus about two hours to see some of the most notable things of the old city. Among the first places where we went was the top of the Castle. The view from this eminence is the most extensive, the most varied, the richest, and too, especially, is some of the most rugged scenery. Both this city and its surrounds are famous for their historical associations. The famous field of Bannockburn is only a few miles to the south, and a great many other of the varied conflicts of the old Kingdom can be pointed out.

We went to see the Drummond Museum, where all the Tart[a]ns of various Highland Clans are kept, and also other Scottish Relics. We had some eating and refreshments, and my friend avowed himself to be a total abstainer. We then went to take our coach journey, but before mounting, he took out his satchel, a Highland Bonnet, putting it on his head and says, "Now I must throw away my hat as it will encumber me when we come to walk."

Among the people standing round the coach was an old beggar woman. He called out to her, "Here, old woman, will you have this old hat?" She looked at him in astonishment and said, "Dear me, sir, how will e do wantin eir hat?" "Never mind," he said, holding it out to her, "I have got this bonnet." She then took it with the most grateful obeisance.

It was a large coach, and the seats were all crowded, both outside and inside. The seats on the top were arranged in pairs, opposite each other. A great many of the travelers on this coach I found to be strangers of various nationalities. On the seat on which my new friend sat, at our right hand was a Frenchman and his wife who could not speak good English. My friend spoke a word to the lady in French, and she seemed perfectly delighted to talk with a stranger in her own language. And for sometime there was nothing to me but a great laughing and gabble in French. On the seat opposite sat two well-dressed ladies with gold rings and other rich trappings. I got into conversation with them, and they seemed to be well educated and in no way reserved. They told me that they were from South Carolina, were intending to visit some of the great places of Europe, and were now taking Scotland on their way. They had friends in Florence, Italy and would probably spend the winter there. I said I understood there

73

were a great many who held slaves in those southern states, and hoped they had nothing to do with that business. This at once brought them out and they boldly confessed that they were slave-owners: and instead of being ashamed, they were rather proud of it, and the more so since they had spent a week or two in Ireland and seen the misery and starvation of the poor working classes of that country. They said that they used all their slaves well, that they had all the comforts of life and were happy, and knew they were kindly treated. They had a great love and respect for their master and mistress. I met these reasons they gave me with arguments that have now overthrown slavery, but they only the more asserted that they were right.

* * *

My new friend had been giving a little attention to my arguments with the ladies, and he also gave his wor[d] against slavery, but they met him with arguments as having a just cause; and so there was quite a hot dispute for a few minutes till some scenery and things by the way called our attention to other things. As we drew near Callender, my friend said that he would dismount from the coach quickly and secure lodgings in the Inn. This I found was a good move, as at this season they are often overcrowded.

That evening after supper in the sitting room, we met with some interesting strangers, among them were some Oxford scholars, with whom my friend had some interesting and learned conversation, thus showing that he was something of a scholar. He having secured a bedroom for us both, we retired to it, but before getting into bed, he had a minute or two of private devotion. I followed the same example and thanked God for the way I had been led through the day, and that I had met with a Christian friend. While in bed, we had some talk on religious subjects and then a good night's rest.

We had arranged to start early in the morning and take the road for the Braes of Balquhidder, where is the grave of Rob

Roy. We went so far up the banks of the Teith through some fine scenery, some of which my friend took a sketch. At one time while he was sketching, I saw among the heather at our feet some fine blaeberries. He never had seen any of them before and I repeated to him the stanza of a song [by Robert Tannahill] which says: 'Let us go lassie go to the braes O Balquhidder, where the blea-berries grown mang the bonnie hill and heather.'

As he looked and saw the way in which they grew among the heather which was then in bloom, he admired the truth and simplicity of the poet as a picture of nature and the beauty of which could be felt till it was seen with the eye. He had a small volume of Scott's *Lady of the Lake* with him, and was reading a descriptive stanza when I took the liberty to correct his Scotch language and read it in the true idiom. He thanked me and said I must now take the book and do the reading.

We went around the foot of the great Ben Ledi. We passed alongside and saw some of the lakes or lochs, as they [are] called such as, Lubnaig, Voil, and Earn. There were wild ravines between with rocky precipices and stream from the mountains rushing down. There was some cultivation of crops in the low grounds, and at one place we went into a house, where we had some good milk and bread; and they refused to take a thing for it. We put some questions to them about church matters and found that they were greatly in favor of the Free Church.

We kept walking on, and I found my friend to be one of the best. He seemed at first to think that I would have some diffi-culty in keeping up with him, but he soon found that he had met his match.

It was sometime in the afternoon when we reached Balquhid-der, romantically situated among the hills and lakes. We looked round the place, saw what was said to be Rob Roy's grave, and had a little rest and refreshments. We then turned toward the south and soon met with a gamekeeper, whom we found to be a man of intelligence, giving us the names of all of the great mountain peaks for 50 miles around. We mentioned we were now on our way for the Trossac[h]s Inn, and he pointed out to us the most direct way.

After going along a high range for some time, we saw a solitary cottage in a glen below. He said he had a great desire to see what sort of people lived in such a place. I said it was not far off our way. On going forward, we met at the door a middle-aged woman who invited us to come i[n]. As we went in we were introduced to a very old lady, whom she said was her mother. She was nearly blind, but her hearing was still pretty good. My friend asked her some questions on religious subjects and she answered him readily and gave evidence that she was well acquainted with the Scriptures. She said when she was young and had her sight, she read the Bible and some other good books, and that she had great happiness now on thinking of these things. He asked her if the Parish Minister ever visited her and she said: "No vera often. We are poor folks and he disna often come this way."

* * *

He then asked her if she would be willing that he should pray with her and she said she would be glad for him to do so. We then engaged in devotional exercises, and he put up a very appropriate prayer for her and her daughter. As he left he gave her half a crown and I gave her a shilling. After we came up to the high ground he expressed his great delight in visiting this humble cottage, and with that he took a sketch of it in his book.

I now stated that I had never asked him where he was from, or what his profession, but now I suspected he was a Clergyman. He at once confessed that he was, and that he would have told me sooner but was afraid that it would have prevented me from expressing myself so freely as I had done on various subjects of our conversation. I said he need have very little fear in regard to that matter. He then mentioned that he was from Wall in England, that his name was Newman Hall, and that he was placed over a Congregational Church in that city, and that he was now on a vacational tour to see Scotland. He mentioned that on the day before he started on this excursion, he spent an hour with Dr. Chalmers and heard some of his plans in organizing the Free Church.

We then pushed on our way, walking at a good pace through some rough grounds. But a good part of it was a downward incline. We arrived at the Trossac[h]s Inn about 8 o'clock, when it was beginning to get dark. We found the house crowded with strangers. The landlord said he could accommodate us with supper and breakfast, but we have to sleep on a cot in one of the sitting rooms.

We therefore had to accept the situation and make the best of it. After having got supper, I found our feet and legs were a little wet in coming through certain pools and long grass, and so I found the way to the kitchen, and in a friendly way asked the cook if she would allow myself and another gentleman to come and have our clothes dried for a few minutes at the kitchen fire. She replied that we should be welcome. I then went to Mr. Hall and told him what I had done, and he at once accompanied me. This gave Mr. Hall an opportunity of seeing a little of high life below stairs. There were a number of servants round, both men and women. We found that a good deal of the talk among themselves was in the [Gaelic] language, but they spoke good English to us. On mentioning that we could not get a bed and would have to sleep in a cot, one of the men suggested that the older gentleman should sleep with the cook and the younger, that was Mr. Hall could have the housemaids. This of course was passed over at the time as a bit of a joke. But Mr. Hall spoke of it to me afterwards that he thought there was too much freedom among those servants, as he observed that these young women rather seemed to favor the suggestion.

The scenery around this Trossac[h]s Inn is truly grand, and on-looking at these, we were led to turn our book and see how graphically Sir Walter had described everything. In passing

77

through the Trossac[h]s, there are two conspicuous mountains on each side. On the right is [Ben Venue], and on the left is [Ben An], rising to the height of two and three thousand feet. In approaching Loch Katrine, we go through a narrow defile for ¾ of a mile, when the whole lake, about 10 miles long, and 2 in breadth. It is said to be 350 feet above sea level, and it now supplies the city of Glasgow with water.

We were taken along it in a large open rowboat, the oarsmen frequently giving us a bit of a song (I see that they have now a Steam Vessel). After arriving at the west end, here were a number of men with ponies to take any across to Loch Lomond. This is a distance of 5 miles, but Mr. Hall and I preferred to walk and were at Inversnaid about the same time as the riders. We had now got into some new scenery. The great Ben Lomond towered up on our left. In front on the west of the lake appears some prominent peaks, called the Alps of Arrochar. This lake is the largest and finest in Scotland, being in length about 30 miles and containing over twenty thousand acres. The whole scenery is varied and beautiful.

We soon saw the steamer coming, and in a little while we were aboard. It then goes up to the north, where the lake gets very narrow. The steamer now turns round, touching at places on each side to take in and let out passengers.

* * *

At Rowerdenn[a]n, on the left, Mr. Hall left the vessel, intending to make the assent of Ben Lomond. I would have gone with him, but had arranged to go to Glasgow. I had a letter from him describing his assent to the top and the extensive view all round. He mentioned also that he preached to an audience on the Sabbath in the open air, being to a party that had left the Established Church. I had also a letter from him shortly after this from the lakes in Westmorland, describing its scenery with some [of] its beautiful lakes and surroundings. But upon the whole, he thought it far behind the rugged scenery of the Trossac[h]s, with its mountains and various surroundings.

I then kept on with the steamer to the end of the lake, and then by way of Dumbarton, and from this on to Glasgow. I stopped there all night, looked around it for a little, and then took the rail to Edinburgh, and in a day or two after this, I was home at Ormiston. I had a very interesting trip, having never seen so much of Scotland before.

Ever since the hot and dry season of 1826, the potatoes had frequently been subjected to a disease commonly known as the Curl in the Shaw. It varied a good deal in some years, being much worse than others. This year, 1843, it was particularly bad and was a great loss to the whole country, especially to the working classes. I noticed that where I had been traveling all through the Lothians and the best lands, this disease was everywhere prevalent, but I noticed that all through the [Trossachs] and the Lake Country, the potatoes were remarkably green and healthy. I asked some of the people if they had ever seen anything of the Curl on their Shaws. They said they had never seen anything of it. This fully confirmed an idea that I had entertained that the disease was principally caused by an over ripening of the Tubers, by which the germination powers of the plant became much weakened.

It so happened that at the Winter Meeting of the Highland Society this year, the great loss that has been sustained by the disease of the Curl in the potatoes was particularly referred as what reason could be given, it was resolved and sanctioned that a prize be awarded by this society to any person who could write an article stating the cause of the disease and a remedy for the same. Here I thought was a chance for me to speak out, and so I at once wrote an essay, giving my experience and observation on the subject and addressed it to the president of the society. I never heard anything more about this till sometime in the summer, the late Dr. Stuart of Kelso being on a visit to Ormiston, and seeing me on an outside border of the garden near the road, he

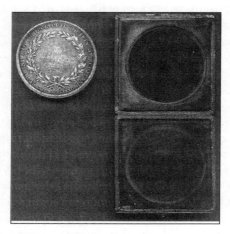

8. Prize medal awarded to George Taylor by the Highland and
Agricultural Society of Scotland in 1844 for his essay on potato curl.

SOURCE: JIM HIGGINS

at once paid me a complement for the high honor I had received
from the Highland Society. I said I was not aware of it. He said
did you not write to them something about a disease of the
potatoes. I said I did sometime ago but had never heard anything
about it. He said that he saw in an Edinburgh Paper this morning
that I had been awarded the Societies Large Silver Medal for a
valuable Essay on the Potato Disease. This was my first notice
but in a day or two after, I had a letter from the president stating
the fact to me, and that I would receive the medal when I called
at the office, giving them my proper initials. This I did and I still
retain it as a momento of Scotland and the Highland Society.

There was another event in my life which occurred about this
time, and this was in a matter of relation to my religious senti-
ments. The Presbyterian Church of Jedburgh of which I had been
a member since 1822, was now thinking of having an addition
to the Eldership. Having mentioned certain districts in which
they were required, it was suggested that the members in these

several places call a meeting for the purpose of nomination one of their member as most fitting for the Eldership. The district of Eckford was one and wanted Thomas Robson, who had been a useful Elder in that place and had just left for America. In the meeting that was called, I was nominated as the most fitting for that office. The next stage of proceeding was for the parties nominated to meet with the minister and elders in the Vestry and to state their willingness to accept office or to give any reason why they could not. I had been thinking over this matter very carefully, and all the more so from the late celebrated trial before the Synod of the Rev. James Morrison of Kilmarnock for heresy. He had ignored the doctrine of a Limited Atonement, had been holding revival meetings, and a great many had been brought to the knowledge of the truth. But then some of the jealous Orthodox had been taking note that he had been doing this not according to the religious standards of the Church, such as the Confession of Faith and the Larger and Shorter Catechisms. So he was the first to be accused of heresy by his Presbytery. The Synod pronounced a sentence against him. He then left with a solemn protest against the action of Synod, and with several other ministers who favored his views, established a religious denomination of their own in Scotland, the Evangelical Union Church, which soon drew to their number a great many from all the other churches.

I now come back to my own case. As I stood in the Vestry before the Minister and Elders at Jedburgh, they seemed to give me a very cordial welcome. But before proceeding, I said I wished to ask them a question or two and it was—if they required from me a verbal assent to the Doctrines of Confession of Faith, especially as they related to that of Election and a Limited Atonement. Here some of the old Greyheads got up and said it was a piece of presumption on my part to question any of these things, and one of them to convince me, took a Testament and read several verses of the 9th chapter of Romans, finishing off with the emphasis: "Jacob have I loved and Esau I hated." In turn I gave them some Scripture reasons for my belief, such as John 3 and 16. The Rev. Mr. Nicol expressed no opinion farther than he was sorry that such a question had been brought up before them. I thus got free from being an Elder and they made no attempt to exclude me as a member of the Church.

It was shortly after this that I was induced to change my situation to that of nursery and seedman. There was a Mr. Andrew Lockie in Kelso, who had long held that situation and for some reason was induced to give it up. Dr. John Stuart had made an arrangement with him to take the business for his brother, who was a writer with a lawyer in the town, but who was often dissipated with drink. He naturally thought that this business might reform him, especially if he could find an active foreman to carry out the business. He thought he had found one in a smart fellow named Black. Together they made a poor combination. And so it was one day in the fall of 1845 the Doctor called upon me at Ormiston and told me all about how matters were going with his brother and Black. He asked if I would undertake to run the business. I said I had never been practiced in the Nursery business and less among seeds, and therefore felt a [diffidence] to undertake such a situation. He said he had no fear for a man who had distinguished himself as a gardener as I had done, and that I should have a good wage and a certain percentage on all the Nursery Stock sold, and if his brother could be kept from drink, he could manage the Seed Store and all the writing correspondence in quite a business manner. I said I would think over the matter for a few days and let him know.

I thought over the matter carefully and prayerfully. I had for the last 10 years, nay I might say 20, been working very hard, and thought this might be easier and bring me into good society. Another inducement was that my brother John, could take the garden at Ormiston along with my mother. I therefore accepted the situation and entered upon it [on] the 1st of February, 1846. My wife and family remained at Ormiston till the 26th of May. At that time I had two children, Isabella and Andrew. I took a house where I had been boarding alongside the Nursery at Forrestfield. It had four rooms with coalhouse and gas. The rent being about ten pounds a year.

The Evangelical Union Church had just been formed the year previous. The minister at that time, the Rev. John Rutherford, a young man, and most devout Evangelist. Revival meetings were being held and a good many from various churches in the Town and Country joined our Union. Several of these Elders and leading members who got new spiritual light ... came boldly out as witnesses for a free Gospel, I joined this body at once. When I came to the town I was cordially received by the Brethren. From the way in which the Church had been formed and was being augmented, it can be easily seen that our little church was looked upon by other churches with very jealous eyes. There were several Baptists and Methodists who at once joined with us. Our only test was a confession of Sin and Faith in the Lord Jesus Christ for Pardoning Mercy. We were in the way also of forming plans of visitation through certain parts of the town, especially in the Sabbath afternoons. We often had Gospel Tracts to give away, and those who were sick, we always gave them a free invitation to come to our Church by this means. We preached the Gospel and were fishers of men.

It was in the year 1845 that the Blight and Potato Rot was first seen in Great Britain and Ireland. I first saw its effects in the fall of that year. The leaves and stems being blighted, and when taken up a few of the tubers were diseased. But after being put in pits a great many rotted. But the next year, 1846, the blight was seen on the Shaws early and many of the tubers began to rot before they had attained their size. The cause of this disease gave rise to great speculation, and the papers were flooded with letters of all sorts of reasons, the most of them, as I soon found, were a great way from the truth. I had formed an opinion from the first that the cause was atmospheric, being aggravated or mitigated according to circumstances. In order to test this I had planted a large quantity of Early Ash Lead Kidney Potatoes, to

meet the demand for customers in spring. I therefore took up
the greater part of these potatoes just as the Shaws were beginning to show blight. I had them put under a large open shed and
covered with mats and straw. In front of this shed, I put down
two bushels of these same potatoes, spreading them out thin in
the shape of two distinct squares. One of these, I covered with
a double thick mat, the other square I left fully exposed to the
sun and atmosphere. In the course of a week, those exposed
began to show a brown decay on the skin, and in the course of
another week, were nearly all rotted. But on taking off the mat
from those alongside, I was agreeably surprised to see every
potato sound and healthy, and I found it also to be the same as
those covered in the shed. I think I had a similar feeling at that
time, as is related of Benjamin Franklin, when with his kite he
had drawn the lightening from the cloud to his feet and seeing
its effect, he exclaimed, "I have found it!" I had left a few of the
same standing in the ground; these I found also to be nearly all
rotted. There was another point thus disclosed in potato and
seed culture; that by taking them up and winnowing them in this
green state, they become greatly strengthened and improved in
their future growth. This was just something of the same in a
varied form, from which I had seen when passing through the
[Trossachs] a few years before and led me to write the essay on the
potato, for which I was awarded a prize by the Highland Society.

I practiced this same method every year with our early seed
potatoes. Our customers found them to be extra good and the
demand greatly increased. It is to be observed however, that this
method applies to the saving of seed potatoes. Those for table
thus require a certain time to mature, in order that starch may
be deposited.

This potato disease of 1846 was very bad in Scotland and
England. I made a tour that year in the month of September
through a good part of Scotland in the way of selling turnip
seeds, and had thus an opportunity of seeing this disease in its
worst form. I saw a great many people foolishly taking them up

and spreading them on the ground in order as they thought to save some. But this disease will be ever memorable as it was manifested in Ireland. The poor people at that time were in a great measure dependent on the potato as chief staple food, and the disease being so bad, nearly the whole crop rotted. This caused a perfect famine in that country and thousands died of starvation. Assistance had to be rendered by the government. America and other countries sent large supplies. There was one thing that this potato disease brought to a speedy termination and that was the abolition of the obnoxious Corn Laws. Sir Robert Peel, the Prime Minister, ... had always been a strong advocate for protection, when the distress of the country caused by the potato disease, and more specifically, the great suffering in Ireland. So soon as a motion was made for the abolition of those laws, he gave his consent, and they were blotted from the Statute Book. This disease has frequently visited the British Isles, but never to the same extent as 1846. They found that some of their best old varieties were most liable to disease, and there has been certain new varieties introduced that more readily resists the atmospheric influence.

In entering on my new business, I found no difficulty in discharging its duties. There was one thing which we just now found to be sort of an "elephant" on our hands, and that was the immense stock of turnip seed. My predecessor, Black, had bargained with the farmers to grow large quantities. A good part of this had been threshed out and cleaned and there were two or three granaries full, and several large stacks yet to thrash, which would call for more storage. This all had to be paid for on delivery. The Doctor mentioned to me that Black had acted foolishly in having engaged so much seed, and which would be a dead stock on hand for some time. He thought therefore that it would be well for me to take a turn through some of the principal parts of Scotland and try to sell part of this seed to dealers at wholesale prices, even if I could get only one or two shillings per bushel more than it cost us. I said I was afraid there would be little demand at present, as Market Quotations were low. He said it would not cost much, only my traveling expenses, and it would let them know at any rate that we had such a stock. So I said I would try what could be done.

I started out on this tour sometime in September, took Edinburgh first, calling on the different Seedsmen. But I could make no sales, though I offered as low as 15 shillings per bushel. Then I went by the way of Dundee and Perth, but they had a supply and none was wanted. Then I went to Stirling and called on Mr. Drummond, but he also was full. It was the same old thing. So I came home and told the Doctor that I could not make any sales. He said the seed would keep for another year or even 2 or 3. But it still had a little more hopeless aspect, as the winter of 1847 was one of the mildest that had been experienced for many years. This had a tendency to preserve the turnips and would favor a large crop of seed for this year.

I shall now refer a little to our church matters and some other things in that connection. We were still adding to our members, and some of these had been pulled out of the dregs (and these being well known in the town), their change of life was a powerful witness that our work was of God. But there were also others, young people of respectable character who were also attracted. I had something to do with one case and it came round in the following manner: Alongside of our nursery were a range of gardens only divided by a hedge 5 feet high. These were either owned or rented by merchants. One of these belonged to a Mr. Adam Nical [Nicol?], who kept a large grocery store. It was his custom to be there early, weeding or planting before breakfast, and in this work he was often assisted by some of his clerks or apprentices. As I was often alongside we had frequent converse, especially with one young man, William Aitken. We had often talked over religious matters and some that had joined our church lately. I urged him also to come and join with us, but he said he could not see his way to leave the old church in which he had been baptized and brought up. I then invited him to come and hear the Rev. William Scott, former minister of his church. Mr. Aitken said he would gladly come. The church that day was crowded to its utmost capacity. It so happened that I was the Pre[c]ent[o]r that day to lead the singing and had a good view of the audience. Among them I saw my young friend. Rev. Scott preached an arousing sermon, in which blended both law and gospel. As this church was dismissing, Aitken came and shook my hand, saying, "Now I see you are right and I feel very happy".

We attended the services of the afternoon and evening, when I introduced him to Mr. Scott, with whom he had considerable conversation. We found afterwards that there had been several other parties aroused by the day's preaching. William Aitken joined our church at once and showed a most devoted spirit in all our prayer meetings, and at the same time showed the greatest diligence in going out and conversing with others. Later in life he devoted all his time to religious work and was one of the party that organized the Young Mens Christian Association in London.

Our church was frequently visited by strangers who might be stopping in town for a time or passing through on a business trip. A very memorable case of this kind occurred to me about the end of 1846. One Sabbath morning I noticed a well dressed gentleman of middle age come into our church and listen very attentively to the sermon. I noticed also that he was at the afternoon and evening services. After church was dismissed I was in the way with another of the Brethren counting the collection. This was taken in two close boxes placed on each side of the entrance. I counted mine and found among the small change two half crowns. I then asked my neighbor, Samuel Dickie, if he noticed that stranger gentleman who had been with us all day. He said he did and was wondering who he was. I said I did not know but wished he would come everyday, for I had two half crowns in my box, and believed they were from him. In the Monday just after I had got dinner and gone out to the nursery, our shop boy, William Mein, came up and said that Mr. Handside, the Nurseryman, was at the Cross Keys Inn, and I was to come down and see him. I went down and found him in the Sitting Room, and received from him a very hearty reception. I was acquainted with this gentleman before, having several times purchased some of his fine Dahlias.

He at once asked me what I would like to drink, I thanked him and said I would rather not take anything at present. But you must he said, and with that rang the bell and ordered some whiskey. We talked over some business and when the whiskey came, I had to take a sip of it. Turnip seed was talked about and he thought it likely that prices would be lower than last season. While we were talking, I was rather surprised to see sitting in another corner of the room, the same gentleman who attended our church yesterday. And I soon perceived he had his eye upon me. As I was about to go away, I noticed that he went out to the door, and after I had bade goodbye to Mr. Handside and had come out to the hall, there was the gentleman standing. There was at once a mutual salute. I mentioned that I thought he was the same gentleman which I saw at our church yesterday, and he said he was. He said he was very highly pleased with our minister and the devoted Christian appearance of the people, and he thought such a church was calculated to do much good, but he said in a feeling way: "Dear Brother, I am sorry to see that you have not joined the Temperance Society. I hope you will soon se[e] it your duty to do so." I said I had no desire for drink, and was well aware that it was a great evil to many, but that I was peculiarly situated in my business as a nursery and seedman, and that it was often necessary in making a sale in that line to treat your customer.

He said he was well aware that this was the habit of the world. But he held it to be the duty of every Christian to witness against such things, that we are our brother's keepers. "Now," he said, "to bring this case home to yourself, you are the third man within the last two hours that has been doing business with this gentleman in the same way, and there is no doubt if he goes on, that in a little time he will die a drunkard. Now, my brother, in that day when we must give an account of all our duties and relations with each other, will you be free of the blood of this man?"

I felt the truth of this. It touched my conscience to the quick, and with emphasis, I said, "God helping, I will give it up." I asked him his name and where he was from; he told me he was a traveler in business for [the] Lord Mayor of London. He gave me a specimen of some Gospel Tracts which he said he always carried for distribution. He was going with the stagecoach to Berwick, and then take the train to Edinburgh.

It was about this time that the first great wave of Temperance came over Great Britain and Ireland. In Scotland the Temperance League was formed and certain agents were appointed to travel and deliver lectures. The wave had also struck Kelso, and several with myself were laboring to promote the course. We had some noted cases to work upon. Among the most prominent was James Hooper Dawson, editor of the *Kelso Chronicle*, a man with all his brilliant talents in advocating political reform, was a slave to drink and was therefore found wallowing in the mire. He was talked and reasoned with, signed the Pledge and became Champion in the cause.

There was also another, Andrew Dun Miller. He spent all the money he could lay hands on for drink, while his wife and family were starving. He was that far gone in the habit that he often saw what they called the "Blue Devils". I was first introduced to him by Robert Rutherford, who was a member of our church. We reasoned and pled with him and got him to sign the pledge. He kept it, became a man, and settled down to business. His sons joined him in the milling and grain business, and now they are the wealthiest firm in that place. The Temperance reform in this way received a great impetus and a Temperance Society was formed. Mr. Dawson was the president and myself vice president. We invited some of the greatest Temperance Lecturers, amongst which was John B. Gough.

I now again come to speak of our nursery business. The winter of 1847 was one of the mildest. Hence a great deal of the turnip crop would not be used, it would be used for seed. This naturally caused a very poor outlook for us. About the end of March, whole fields could be seen standing about, coming into bloom. Then a cold spell came over the fall of snow. Following this there was night of moist frost, and as vegetation had been prematurely advanced, it met with a thorough check and kill.

I hastened down to our seed store and found our boy Archie rubbing his hands and with a wry face, saying what an awful morning it was. I said, "Well however you may feel, it has been a grand night and morning for us." He did not understand my meaning, when I said the cold night had killed all the growing turnip seed. I told him that I had been examining Mr. Tait's patch and found it thoroughly destroyed. That day the papers mentioned that the frost had been most severe over the whole country and that especially the growing turnip seed had been destroyed. "Now," I said to Mr. Stuart, "you will have a number of letters asking about our turnip seed and our prices, but don't commit yourself for a little while."

This just happened so, and for a time we were flooded with letters. He answered those parties by saying, "We have a very large stock of fine turnip seed but have not yet made up our minds as to the price. Our foreman will call upon you in a few days, when prices will be submitted." I talked the matter over with the Doctor, and as there was yet a great uncertainty as to the price, I said that when I started, I would first go to Edinburgh and call upon Mr. Lawson, the leading seedman in Scotland to ascertain what he thought might be the price. This I did and had a considerable talk with him. He said that since the crop of that year had been destroyed, there were many rumors and talk about prices and some of them were very extravagant. He said there was no doubt that prices would be much higher than ever before, that he had decided to make his retailing price two shillings per pound, and as he would require a considerable stock to supply customers he would give me an order for 100 bushels at 75 shillings per bushel. This I knew was a great difference of that I had been offered at only 15 shilling. I accepted his offer, and signed the contract. I then called on other seedmen of that city and showed them Mr. Lawson's order. In this way all my sales afterward became a very simple matter. I then went to Dundee and made large sales, also at Perth and Stirling.

While waiting at the station for the Glasgow train, I was agreeably surprised to meet with my old friend who tackled me on the Temperance question at Kelso. I was surprised that he knew I was carrying out my Temperance pledge. He said he knew because that night when he prayed, he had at once a most assured confidence that his prayer would be answered. He asked me if Temperance had hurt my business, and I told him about our good luck. "Thank God!" he said, "That is another answer to prayer for in that connection with Temperance, I prayed also that the Lord would bless and prosper you in all business relations." Thus was our meeting terminated by the train coming along, he going in the other direction.

After visiting Glasgow and making sales, I came home by the way of Edinburgh and spent part of the day with my sister Mary. On coming home I had a hearty reception from the Doctor and his brother. The seed put our firm in the higher position and enabled us to carry out our nursery business on a more extensive scale.

The extension of the Railroad at this time and certain things in necessary connection with it, gave an impetus to the nursery business for certain things wanted. Among the first was young Hawthorne quicks. But as other nurseries had an oversupply, the price was often less than cost. Another thing railroads brought into requisition was the Larch Tree for railroad ties. This induced all landed proprietors to plant a great number of these trees on waste lands. I spoke to Mr. Stuart that I thought we ought to put out a good number of Larch. He thought it might be well but not too many, considering the Hedge Trade had been a failure. I knew of a piece of land with reasonable rent adapted to these trees. He said for me to make a trial of it. This I did. I ordered two year seedlings from Mr. John Reid at 18 pence per 1,000. The trees were carefully planted and cultivated through the summer and were fine stock in the fall. I advertised them in the London papers as being adapted for estate plantations. In a very little while we had a letter from a gentleman of Kent and he wished us to send to his address 31,000 Larch trees. Mr. Stuart was proud of such a large order and he hoped I would send our best trees. I though[t] it would be better to send to Mr. Reid in Edinburgh to take up and pack in crates for us our large order and have them shipped by sea to the address in Kent. This piece of business wrought well and left us with a good profit, and the gentleman was well pleased with his trees, procuring us several other orders from his neighbors. We had a good many orders from gentlemen nearer home.

We also made a good deal from our nursery in the floral and ornamental departments. Certain new varieties of flowers were being brought out, and at the various meeting[s] of our Horticultural Society there was often keen competition. There were several amateurs in the town who were quite enthusiastic in this way, speaking to obtain every new variety that came out. This had the effect to stir up the gardeners of the various gentlemen in the neighborhood. We had a long and broad gravel walk in the midst of our nursery with tall growing plants, as Hollyhocks, Dahlias, Standard Roses, and some of the new flowering shrubs. Nearer to the walk were many varieties of roses, and next to the box edging were all the finest Annuals, which were then making their first appearance from California. This became a great pleasure walk for all parties, especially for those who were fond of flowers. It also afforded me a fitting opportunity to show off to the best advantage any new variety of flowering plant, which had met with the highest commendation from London Horticultural Society. Such parties were often asking a great many questions about such plants. Often it resulted in a large order.

Some of those new varieties of flowers and plants were offered to the public at first at very high prices, but in order to carry out our business, it was necessary that we should have them. I had some difficulty with our boy Archie on some of these things. New roses being all the rage, a variety called Queen Victoria came at 10 shillings and sixpence each. The company had such demand for this rose; they could only send us sleeping buds, two for a guinea. One of these buds did not develop, but from the other I was able to bud 27 from it and every one grew. I sold a good many of the strongest of these for 5 shillings. Archie had thought the guinea wasted at first.

Our Horticultural Society increased in prosperity. Mr. Stuart was chosen secretary and did all the writing in that connection, while I made the arrangements of the Hall and the various things exhibited. We divided into two classes: one for the Gentleman Gardeners, and the other for amateurs. This gave the latter the privilege of showing in the first class, and we found that this had the effect of stirring up much greater emulation. It was also my endeavor to make a good display at these meetings from our Green House and Nursery. All new roses, Hollyhocks, and Dahlias were always shown to the best advantages. When the ladies came round and were admiring such things, I was always there to answer questions, and often got good orders. I was in the way also of attending some of the adjacent—such as Jedburgh, Hawick, Berwick, and Coldstream. I was often called up to act as a judge. I brought a box of special flowers with me, bringing something before the public in order to make a sale. In going about in this way, I met all the gentleman gardeners and many amateurs in horticulture. I also got well acquainted with all the farmers in the district, as it was my business to sell all the various seeds they might require, such as turnip, clover, and grass seeds.

There was another thing which came up in our line of business at this time, which was the sale of certain farm manure— bone dust and guano. Both of these were found most efficient in improving the growth of the turnip crops. Mr. Stuart's brother-in-law, Mr. John Roberton, who was farmer at [Ednam

Farm], a little below Kelso, had got up a mill especially for grinding bones. Many people made a business of collecting and bringing them to Mr. Roberton. I think he paid them 5 pence per stone of 14 pounds. He got his main supply from towns and cities by the railroad. We were his agents to sell those ground bones and had a large house in town on the banks of the Tweed, where they were stored and ready for sale. This was not a pleasant business, for the bones in a large heap emitted a smell. Soon we had collected all the rats in the neighborhood, but we soon found a method of turning this Charnel House into a trap for catching rats. On one side were open windows with blinds, where rats could readily come. These were often so constructed that they could be shut from outside in a few seconds. The only entrance was through several open latticed windows on [the] opposite side, and this was upon a perpendicular wall of 12 feet on the banks of the Tweed. I told this to some who had Terrier dogs and they upon told others, and I have seen more than a dozen assembled to have a hunt. The first process was to shut the windows on one side, then the parties with their dogs standing at each end of the building on the bank of the river. Then the door at the end opened, and when parties rushed in with long sticks pounded the bones and the rats who had to make their escape, leaped out through the open slats into the river. And there was such a scene of splash and worry and felling with long sticks which for some time made quite an exciting scene. I think I have seen as many as 100 rats at once.

Another thing in connection with this bone manure was sulfuric acid. It was found that this ingredient, when mixed with broken bones, reduced them to a fine dust, and a small quantity of this sown along the drill produced a superior crop of turnips. This article was also sold and it came in large glass bottles, called Carboys (which weighs 150 lbs.). It was just a little before this that Guano came to be known as manure, and we sold great quantities of it. One great advantage of this concentrated manure, was the ease in which they could be applied and their immediate effect on the crop. The first time I found this out was on a piece of land of about two acres. From this [a] crop of Hawthorne plants had been taken. This ground was ploughed without any manure and a crop of potatoes was planted in rows with a dibble 2 ½ feet apart. After they came up, so as to show where the rows were, I sowed along these a very light sprinkling of Guano, which seemed to have an immediate effect, as the shaws assumed a dark, bushy growth and a fine crop of potatoes was the result. This, I more fully tested by leaving a row or two without the Guano. These were stunted and growth with yellow shaws and a poor crop of small potatoes.

After taking a prominent part in the Temperance cause, it naturally brought me into acquaintance with many of the best people of the town, and then we found that there were certain other evils that required attention. There were two of these— the opening of the Post Office and running of Railway Trains on the Sabbath Day. One of the most prominent Clergymen in Kelso at that time was the Rev. Horatious Bon[a]r. He warmly took up the subject and preached some sermons about it. A delegation of two from the various churches were drafted to meet together and discuss the matter. It was therefore resolved and adopted that Tracts bearing on the subject should be distributed to every house in the town and neighborhood.

I think it was about 1848 or 1849 that Cholera again visited the British Islands. It was very malignant in Kelso. I noticed that in many of the fatal cases were those who were addicted to drink, and some with a weak habit of body. I have seen some perfectly well and in 6 hours they were corpses. There was no doubt that it was an atmospheric disease, and that it was also infectious. Of this I had a notable instance in a young man whose name was Dalgliesh, drayman at Kelso Mill. He was suddenly seized and died. Notice of his death was sent to his parents who lived 6 miles in the country. One of our seed graineries was adjacent to the mill, and I was just coming from it in the morning when I met Simon Dalgliesh and his burial. After they went home they were seized with cholera and died. Another thing I found peculiar in this disease was that it followed a good deal along the course of the rivers. There were two cases on the Teviot with which I was well acquainted. One was a Robert Heron, a tailor at Kale Waterfoot,[9] which was fatal, and the other case was that of my mother at Ormiston Garden. A special message was sent to me that my mother was ill. I went at once and found her very weak, but the doctor said the disease had taken a turn which gave some symptoms of hope. And so it was, for she soon got better. There were also several other cases alongside the Teviot.

Mr. John Rutherford left our church about a year after I had joined it, and did some Evangelical work in other places. Most of the preachers that followed were young men and boarded at my house. We ultimately called a permanent pastor, a Mr. James Howrie, a native of Ayrshire. He was married and had a family and did some good work in our church. Our mode of support was voluntary, each giving in accordance to their ability; and it wrought well. But we had also some trials in our church connections. A Baptist preacher created much strife and drew away all our Baptists converts. Some of our Brethren were very intolerant with those who had been Immersed. I saw the danger and took a stand between parties, advising Toleration and forbearance, but the feeling ran high and I was in the way of getting a little bit of a kick from each. This state of matters continued until the party formed a church. But after struggling for a year or two they had to disband.

From the movement that had been made in Kelso for better observance of the Sabbath, it was resolved that a prize of five pounds be given for the best essay on the Sabbath, and two pounds and ten shillings be given for the second best. The Sabbath essay was confined to working men in counties of Roxburgh and Berwick. I tried my hand and sent in an essay. I was so far gratified in being awarded the first prize, and I have no doubt it would have been printed, if I had belonged to a more fashionable church. I have however a manuscript copy in a book.

I had frequent letters from my brothers James and Andrew in America, that they were getting along well. The year 1851 will always be famous, as that in which the first great World Fair was held in London. In the opening of that year I had a letter from James, saying that he and his wife were intending to make a visit to see all the friends and the World Exhibition. This was realized, when he and his wife arrived at our house in Kelso about the end of May. I had a good time visiting round with him, and he seemed to look at some of the proud farmers and landlords with a little disdain. Among others he visited John Park of Wooden, who gave him the kick that made him go to America. He said to Mr. Park that he had called to thank him as one of his best friends in being the first means of bringing him to America, where he had now 400 acres of land of his own, besides other house property. I have no doubt Mr. Park accepted this as a sort of left-handed compliment, but it went to show that there was a Divine Power overruling all things for good.

It was sometime in the month of July when he thought to go and see London and the Exhibition. As I had never seen London before, I thought I would go with him. And so with his wife, we took an Excursion Train from Edinburgh. This train started on the Saturday evening, causing us to travel a part of the way on the Sabbath, which, in other circumstances, I would have avoided, but I made the best of it by distributing Tracts and talking with some parties on religious subjects. We arrived at the great city in the forenoon. I had a map and a guidebook with me which I had previously studied, and so I took a Hack at the station which took us and our baggage to Bow Lane, Cheapside, where our Hackman said he could get us lodgings with a lady in a comfortable way and at a lower rate than we expected. After having dinner and a rest, I proposed to my brother to take a walk out and see a little of the city. He said he was afraid we would lose ourselves. I said I had no fear, but that I could travel by the map over the whole city. So we started down Cheapside by the bank and Leadenhall to the end of the bridge. On going down to the Thames, here we saw vessels of all sorts, going up and down. And just at the wharf, where we were standing, was one of the steamers that was to start in a few minutes for Chelsea, about 3 or 4 miles sail up the river. Perhaps there was no other way in which a stranger could see so much of the city in so short a time. There was one place on the way up most peculiar at this time—that was from the London Bridge and two miles upward w[h]ere the Thames Embankment now is. At that time you could see nothing but ragged gable ends and warehouses. Now the fine Boulevard and ornamental grounds in front presents a scene of beauty and variety. Our vessel passed other crafts of all sorts and sizes, while the water of the river seemed a sort of mud puddle. The river takes a winding course when passing along by the Vauxhall Gardens and the new Houses of Parliament. On coming up [to] Chelsea, the view opens up considerable to the north and where at that time could be seen the Crystal Palace in Hyde Park. After leaving the steamer, we took a sort of a beeline for the great building. We had a look at it from the outside, as it was not open on Sundays. Then we took our way down to what is called Rotten Row, past Apsley House, then occupied by the Duke of Wellington, then along Piccadilly to the foot of Regent, then down by the way of Trafalgar Square, the Strand, Fleet Street, Ludgate Hill, round St. Paul's Cathedral, and to our lodgings in Bow Lane.

We spent over 14 days in and around this great city. Of course the Exposition was most attractive, and being the first time the world had ever brought its various productions together. Some great men were also to be seen, such as the Duke of Wellington and Prince Albert, and also Queen Victoria at certain times. I visited Kew Garden and Sion House, the beauties of which I could appreciate. One day brother James and I went out to Windsor Castle and were permitted to walk through the principal rooms of the palace. Then in the park adjoining was held at that time the great Agricultural Show of the Royal Society in which the finest stock of all various sorts were exhibited. There was also a very large and elegant pavilion where there was to be a great dinner in honor of Prince Albert. We learned he would make his appearance in a Royal Carriage. We saw a great crowd gathering and so pushed down among them. I recollect brother James, in order to have a good view, contrived to perch on one of the stone pillars of the gate. In a little time his Royal Highness appeared sitting in an open carriage, and graciously acknowledging the honors done him.

I spent one or two very interesting days in the British Museum, and the first day that I went was something more than ordinary interesting. I had seen in the paper the evening before that a ship load of Niniveh Marbles had arrived at Portsmouth and would be brought to the museum right away. So I thought I would spend a day there anyway. It so happened that when I went in, there was an immense crowd, all round about. The marbles had arrived and they were just in the act of carrying them in. It struck me afterwards on reading the Prophecy of Nahum on the Destruction of Nineveh how very literally I had seen that prophecy fulfilled. Not only does this prophet speak of this city being buried in her grave and become vile, but also about being raised up to become grazing stock to the nations. This was very literal[ly] that day, as all the nations of the earth were then represented in London.

In the time I was in London I visited many of the great sights in and around the city, such as the Old Tower, the shipping docks, and Thames Tunnel. There is a vast amount of history associated with all these. The Regent Park with the Menagerie of the great variety of animal life is highly interesting. Another great sight was Madame Tassards [Tussauds] great historical collection of famous men and women of the world: there you see them standing dressed, as they were living.

In the great Exhibition, the various industries of all the nations were fully displayed. In the American Department, though not a large display, there were some things that attracted great attention. My brother's wife had often been telling us about their

American cooking and heating stoves, and how much they were superior to our open fires. When we first came into this department she at once directed my attention to their stoves. First by opening the iron door and showing how wood was put in, then with a handle taking off the circular covers and placing on a pot or kettle. There were ovens for roasting or baking, and above a fountain for a constant supply of hot water. While she was showing off this and talking, a great crowd of people were soon attracted and many questions were asked and answered. Another thing in this department which attracted by far the greatest attention was the McCormack Reaping Machine. This was the first time it had been shown in England, and was always surrounded by a crowd. When harvest came on, several were put in operation in various places and were witnessed by thousands. But at that time it was a very plain affair to what it is now with all its various apparatus for cutting, gathering, and binding.

There were also some great meetings held in London at this time. I attended two of these in Exeter Hall. One of these was for the purpose of forming a National Alliance to settle all disputes that might arise and so prevent war. Mr. Cobden and a French[man] Emile de Gerardine were the principle speakers. They enunciated some great truths and passed some resolutions which have scarcely ever been acted on except in the case of the *Alabama*.[10] The other meeting that I attended was also philanthropic. Its principle object was a protest upon the evils of slavery. Some things were said about the strange anomaly of the American Government. Elihu Burritt, the learned blacksmith was a principal in this meeting and some Americans from the south were very much disgusted.

I think it might be necessary at this time in 1851 to give some account of my family relations and their places of residence. My oldest sister Mary was married to a Robert Stevenson who was a baker in [Crailing]. About 1824 he lost in business and they went into Edinburgh, where he had difficulty for some time in finding employment. They made a shift to get along by keeping some of the student boarders. Then Robert got [a] permanent situation in a large confectionery store. Their family consisted of one girl till Andrew, their only son was born in 1820[?]. The girl died from scarlet fever. Andrew went to school and used to come out and spend a few weeks with friends in the country, and then served an apprenticeship of 5 years as bookseller. His father died, and in 1852 or 1853 he commenced bookseller on his own account at the same place, where he is still at No. 9 North Bank Street.

My second sister Agnes was married to William Huggan about 1833 [or 1830]. His trade was millwright and he had just commenced business on his own account and seemed successful. He bought a piece of steep property on what was called the Abb[e]y Bank and by cutting in and leveling down, got as much land, where he built a good dwelling house and a large range of work shops. About this time they had a large family of sons and daughters.

Alexander, my oldest brother, was married in 1829 to Isabella Robson. For two years he wrought at laboring work, where he could find it, but in a little time engaged as Farm Steward to Mr. William Purvis, farmer. There, he brought up a large family, mostly daughters, where they were all well employed for a time on the farm. The management of the farm was greatly entrusted to Alexander.

I pass over brother James' history, as it has been already related and also that of Andrew, who had settled and was doing well in Kalamazoo. My youngest sister Margaret was married about 1843 to a George Telfer of Jedburgh, a cabinetmaker, [who] was considered a good expert at his business but was apt at times to be led away by social companions into dissipation, which sometimes caused an unpleasant feeling in the family.

My youngest brother John left the garden at Ormiston about 1850 for the situation of gardener at Hartrigge near Jedburgh. This extensive estate had lately been purchased by Lord Campbell, then Lord Chief Justice of England. The garden had to be remodeled and laid out anew, and I recollect I was in the way of rendering John some assistance in this matter, and also in laying out some new drives in the park. I also supplied from our Kelso nursery a great many fruit trees for the garden and some of the finer sort of shade trees for the park. My mother also left Ormiston and took a house at Bongate, where she was close beside John and her other married daughters, Agnes and Margaret, where she was always a welcome guest.

I was now getting into a family myself. I had their names and births all registered in a book. The first is Isabella Taylor born at Ormiston Parish of Eckford December 10th, 1842. The next is Andrew Taylor born at Ormiston December 20th, 1844. Next James A. Taylor born at Kelso, April 15th 1849. Then Violet Stevenson Taylor born at Kelso January 24th, 1852. George Taylor born Kelso February 4, 1847.

It will be seen from what I have above mentioned that brother James and his wife had a large circle of friends to visit. It was a pleasant time with all parties, and so they left for home about the end of August. I mentioned to James that it was my intention to come out to America and start a nursery, and as I had sent 100 dollars with Andrew to purchase land, I hoped he would have it ready for me whenever I came, and that 10 acres of good land would be enough. He thought a nursery to raise fruit trees would pay well, as they were in the way of purchasing all such from eastern dealers, but that there was no need for Evergreen and Forest Trees, as they had far more of these than was wanted. I therefore remained in the Kelso Nurseries till 1855.

Since a Temperance Society had been formed in Kelso with James Hooper Dawson as president and me vice president, we kept the subject before the people by having frequent lectures by prominent leaders in that cause. The Scottish Temperance League was formed and it sent out agents who frequently visited the southern district [such as] George Easton. He was from a peasant family in Liddiesdale, and having joined the Temperance Society, he began to talk on the subject, and with so much acceptance that he was appointed one of the League's agents. It was at that time that the celebrated John B. Gough made his first visit to Scotland and England. When he came to Edinburgh I recollect Mr. Dawson and I both went in to hear him. The meeting was in the music hall with a crowd of about four thousand. It was quite common at that time to begin such meetings with what was called a soiree or swarie as it was spoken. This consisted of tea and coffee with varieties of bread and cake. This meeting was conducted in this way. On entering, you purchased a ticket for sixpence or shillings. Then you are handed a cup and saucer. You pass into the hall and find a seat. Then when the house is full, tea and coffee is served by parties coming around with a tea and coffee pot in each hand. You hold your cup and get a supply of what you name. Other parties follow with trays of bread and cake, so that you can take what you please. When you get through, there are parties ready to take your cup and saucer. The whole of this vast assembly were served in the way I have described in half an hour. After the leaders had made some remarks, Mr. Gough was introduced to the audience. His manner seemed rather diffident at first, but he soon warmed up, and for an hour and a half, kept the audience spellbound, as he portrayed the effect of drunkenness.

There is no doubt that the thrilling lectures inducted a great many to join the Temperance Society, but it is evident that so long as the root of the evil remains, that is license and is under the fostering care of the government, so will drunkenness abound. At that time it was quite common to see farmers and tradesmen who regularly attended the Kelso Market on Fridays going home drunk. There were instances of lives being lost in this way, I have seen more than once some of the ministers of the gospel going home in this way. One noted this was on the Monday after the sacrament at Ednam. I was downtown that evening, sitting on the steps of Johnston the Saddler. Along with some others, when we saw three riders come into the market square from Union Street. We soon perceived they were the worse of drunk, and as they came nearer, I saw they were ministers and knew them all. It was a sad sight, and went to show the great necessity for reformation beginning in the house of God.

While I resided in Kelso, I had sometimes occasion to call upon that wealthy and benevolent lady, Mrs. Robertson of Ednam House.[11] When there was any charitable movement and subscription were being taken, I was always deputized to visit this lady. She was always so cheerful and seemed to have a pleasure in giving. It was about this time that she made a present to the town of that fine piece of ground known since as Shedden Park. I was deputized to lay out the ground with walks and shrubbery and I think I also planted a Beech Hedge all round it. The main entrance was by a high arched gate, and I suggested to the lady that some large trees planted on each side of this arch would be good accompaniment. And I mentioned that there were some in the Duke's Park which required thinning out were the very thing for this purpose. In a day or two the Duke's Forester called upon me and said I was to go with him and select whatever trees I wanted. This I did and then set about a plan to move and plant them, so they would grow. I had just been reading sometime before how a gentleman in the west of Scotland had moved a great many trees of 30 and 40 feet high with success. This was by digging a deep circle a good way from the center of the tree and then digging and working inwards, taking care as you proceed to tie up and preserve all the roots and fibers. Then having a large trunk or carriage with wheels to pull the tree down upon when it could be drawn to the plane wanted, where a suitable place had been prepared for planting. I went to this work in the way mentioned and it created quite a sensation to the people in the town in seeing such large trees drawn along their streets. I think we moved 6 trees in this way and they all grew and gave at once to the entrance a finished appearance.

In the time that I was in Kelso that connection of the railroad was made from Edinburgh by way of Galashiels, Melrose, St. Boswells, and Roxburgh. Here the most natural and easy way would have been to bring it down the side of the Teviot and crossing the Tweed above the Chalkheugh, cross over Roxburgh Street, and then leading by the way of the Inch Park to the north of Forrestfield. Here would have been brought direct into town instead of being carried round by the way of [Maxwellheugh]. Now why was this not done? The very simple reason was that it would have come to near the grounds and policy of the Duke of Roxburgh. Kelso was left in her beauty and gentility, while the neighboring towns got the business and wealth resulting from a direct rail connection.

4

To America

I THINK it was about 1853 that I had a letter from my brother Andrew stating how he was getting on [in] his business, also mentioning that he had bought 140 acres of land near the town and that he had been preparing to have some of it put into wheat, and that whenever I or any of the friends should come, we should have whatever we wanted for a nursery. I thought over the matter carefully. I was at present in a good situation for myself, but then I was getting into a family and what future prospect was there for them. I naturally thought as my brothers had done so well, I had surely as good if not a better chance than they. I therefore gave notice to Mr. Stuart as to what my intentions were and that my services would terminate on the 26th of May. He said he regretted very much that I should leave, but could not blame me for doing better. I thought I would arrange my affairs so as to sail sometime in the month of August. As Mr. Stuart had got no person to fill my place, I was in the way of doing some nursery work through the course of June and July and early August. I fixed on a day of sale for my books and household furniture. This came round in a favorable way; the various articles being sold for pretty fair prices.

A little previous to this, I had a tribute of respect and grateful remembrance paid me from two different bodies in which I had been much identified in Kelso. The first was from the church with which I was connected, and I shall here transcribe the report as it appeared in the *Kelso Chronicle* of August 3, 1855:

"At the conclusion of the Services in the Evangelical Union Church, a special meeting was held, when the Rev. William Allan in a few appropriate remarks presented Mr. Taylor with a handsome Bible in name of the brethren bearing the following inscriptions, 'Presented to George Taylor, Elder by the Evangelical Union Church of Kelso Scotland as a token of respect for his character, his attachment to Christ Cause and his zeal in advancing the interests of the Redeemer's Kingdom in this place, Kelso 25 of July, 1855.' It mentions that Mr. Taylor made a feeling and suitable reply."

The other tribute that I received was from the Total Abstinence Society and appeared in the *Kelso Chronicle* in the same connection which is as follows:

"Mr. George Taylor, Nurseryman, being about to leave this country for America, was entertained on Saturday Evening by the members of the Kelso Total Abstinence Society and other friends in Mr. Rutherford's Temperance Hotel here. The company set down to tea about eight o'clock and spent a harmonious and happy evening. All present wishing Mr. Taylor health and happiness in the Country of his adoption. In the course of the evening testimony was borne to regard and esteem entertained by all for Mr. Taylor in the various efforts made by him for the advancement of the moral and social good of those around him, and a copy of Mr. Dawson's *Statistical History of Scotland* was presented to Mr. Taylor, bearing the following inscription, 'Presented to Mr. George Taylor on his leaving for America by J. Hooper Dawson, President of the Kelso Total Abstinence Society, Kelso 28 of July, 1855'."

This book I still have in my library and I find it of great use in reference to Statistics in Scottish History. The Bible, I'm sorry to say, was lost when the Presbyterian Church in Kalamazoo was burned in 1883.

I moved from Kelso on Saturday [18th] of August [1855]. Besides myself and wife, I had 3 sons and 2 daughters. My eldest daughter, Isabella being nearly 13. We had also a good deal of boxes and baggage with us which altogether involved me a great deal of responsibility. We went to our friends at Bonjedward and remained until Monday morning. We started pretty early with our cart and baggage to catch the railway train at Clarilaw which goes to Edinburgh. There we spent the day, taking the evening train to Liverpool. I had a good deal of trouble in getting our baggage transferred from one train to another, as there was no checking as we have in America. We traveled all night and got into Liverpool about 8 o'clock in the morning. I had previously engaged my passage at Kelso. The agent was Mr. Andrew Murray, Foreman in the *Kelso Chronicle*, with whom I was very intimate. The name of the vessel in which we were to sail was the *John Bright*, one of the best, having made some of the quickest runs across the Atlantic of any other sailing vessel. We were also recommended to a certain Lodging House by Mr. Murray, and so we found it out and had comfortable lodgings. I called on the agent and he said we must be all on board the next day. This was quite an easy matter with my family, but our baggage had not arrived and I had rather an anxious time till it came with the afternoon train. I engaged a Drayman to take it down to the dock and then it had to be carried into the ship. Both the Drayman and those carriers made extortionate charges but I had to submit. The ship was moved out to the harbor and loaded with iron and other goods.

We set sail on Thursday evening the 23rd, being towed so far out by a steamer. We passed a pretty good night, and as soon as it was light in morning I was out on deck looking around. There was a fair sidewind and the ship was going a good pace. I could see the Welsh Coast away to the south on the left, and on the right and to the west was Ireland. I felt a good deal interested on looking at the Green Isle for the first time and some beautiful hills at a distance, which they said was the Wicklow Mountains. My family was feeling comfortable below in the berth, but I preferred to remain on deck. We seemed still to be coming nearer the Irish Coast and everything seemed pleasant, when all at once the ship gave an awful shake and lurch. I could not at first understand the cause of this, but the captain and the sailors knew. Our ship had grounded and there we stuck. The sailors were in an awful bustle but they were in hope that the ship would get off when the tide rose, about 11 or 12 o'clock. When there was no prospect of moving they commenced to lighten the ship by throwing out a great quantity of the iron bars they had taken on at Liverpool. They also let out the great casks of water but still no movement. I could now perceive by the way the captain and seamen were acting that some new effort was being made in the way of hoisting sails.

Meantime I took a walk up the hind part of the deck, and thinking and looking at our perilous position, I earnestly prayed that the Lord would look upon us in mercy and bless the means that were being used for our deliverance, and I had a most happy feeling that my prayer would be answered. It was now two o'clock. The wind seemed to increase and the ship began to be toped and swayed, when with a lurch it seemed as thrown over on one side. Then I noticed the prow went round then there was a cheer from the seamen and the vessel was turned with its prow to Liverpool. I felt truly thankful to God for this deliverance. But we were not yet out of danger for it was ascertained there was a great leak, there being 3 ¼ feet of water in the hold. The pumps were at once set. Alternating, one requiring 10 men to work it and we passengers had all to stand in and take our turn. Thus with the other pumps working brought out a stream of water that would have drove a mill. Yet with all this pumping effort the water had risen to 7 ¼ feet in the hold. We thus spent a day and a night in the deepest anxiety, but upon the whole had great reason to thank God for deliverance. There was no doubt but this disaster was caused by running too near the Irish Coast. This vessel having got a fame for making quick passage, the captain instead of tacking to the south, which would have caused delay, kept straight on, and hence the accident.

A steam vessel met us with Mr. Gion the main agent on board. He expressed great sympathy for us passengers, assuring us that we would be kept free of all expenses till another ship was ready for sail. All our luggage was taken out and safely deposited at the dock. We were instructed to take lodgings till Monday morning, when another ship would be provided, when we would be supplied with rations the same as if we were sailing. We thus rested on the Sabbath and we really needed it. On the Monday morning Mr. Norris, one of the agents, took me down to their dock and showed me the vessel that was first to sail, the *Oswego*. This was an older vessel and comparatively small. Mr. Norris said as a friend he would advise me to wait till the *Cultivator* sailed on the first of September. This was in every way like the *John Bright*, being built in New York by the same parties. He then showed me through this vessel and the Berths, and I could now choose one for myself and party, get all our luggage in and wait till the ship sailed. This we did and spent a pleasant week looking round the great shipping docks and the city.

On Saturday the 1st of September, we were moved out into the river, while leading was being taken in. In this way we continued till Tuesday 4th, when we were taken out with a steamer for about 20 miles. We had here a fine view of the Welsh Coast, Hollyhead and hills alongside. That of Ireland could only be seen at a great distance. We had pretty fair sailing for 2 ½ days, when we got out the Irish Channel, pass Cape Clear and out into the main ocean. There was a certain amount of rations daily given out to us, and we had to see to the cooking and boiling ourselves. This gave us a good deal of trouble and some things not very pleasant. We had good sailing till the 8th, when we were becalmed for 2 or 3 days. On the Sabbath 9th, there was an expression by several of the more devout for us to have some form of religious services. This wish was expressed to the captain, who was most willing that it should be so, but as there seemed to be no clergymen on board, we could arrange that I should conduct the meeting. The day was calm and pleasant and we met on the deck in front of the cabin about 11 o'clock.

I commenced by giving out the 100 Psalm and it was well sung being aided by an Irish Protestant family who had learned music and took the different parts. After reading a portion of Scripture and prayer I addressed the audience from 1st Timothy, 2 Chapter and 5th verse. "For there is one God and one mediator between God and men, the man Christ Jesus who gave himself a ransom for all." There was a large attentive audience but a good many of the Roman Catholics kept at a distance. It is truly pitiful to see how these poor creatures are kept and enslaved in ignorance by their priests who have taught them a form of Godliness without the power.

After the meeting an Englishman from Norfolk came forward and shook me warmly by the hand as a Christian Brother. He then showed me a certificate from the religious body he had left. It bore that his name was Watson and that he was a local preacher in Wesleyan Methodist connection highly recommending him to any Christian Brethren in America. I found this man like all his brethren ready to go to work and it was agreed that he should address the meeting in the afternoon. This he did and after introducing the service by singing some of the Methodist hymns and prayer, he gave an address from the 9th chapter of St. Matthew, 6, and brought out some arousing thoughts which were calculated to arrest the careless and stir up the people of God to more zeal and devotion. This man was by trade a carpenter, and he had a very singular family connection on board, nothing less than 4 generations in a parental line. There was first the old great grandfather of 84 who looked stout and healthy, there was his son a stout man but beginning to grey, next the son of the above, then he had a young family on board. I do not know if ever such a family crossed the Atlantic in one vessel before.

We had religious services every Sabbath on our voyage, alternately conducted by Mr. Watson and myself. When the weather would not permit on deck we had it in the first and second cabin.

* * *

I had a good deal of trouble with my wife, especially in the early part of our voyage, when the ship gave a great pitch and rolled over she got so excited. The girl Agnes Ker who was with us was very little better. All my reasoning had no effect. It hurt themselves and had also a bad effect on the children.

From the 9th till the 22nd, we were a good deal becalmed, and when there was wind it was often [ahead]. The first severe storm we had was on the 19th. I noticed in the morning a circle round the sun, such as is sometimes seen on land about midday. The wind rose and for 5 or 6 hours blew very hard. It was also a good deal ahead of us, but what was a most singular thing, it stopped blowing all at once. But though the wind had ceased the waves seemed only to rise higher and rolled in such a way as made the great ship rock and roll from side to side, like a huge cradle in such a way that many thought she would turn over altogether. It had a most fearful effect in the interior of the vessel, for it so happened that a great many of the chests and boxes had not been lashed, and a number of them rolled over from one side of the ship to the other. The water came and slop pails were overturned and kept up a rattling and clattering with the movement of the ship. It was difficult for any person to preserve their centre of gravity, and some severe falls were got. What with the shrieking of women and the cries of children and the rattling of tins and boxes, it was a scene altogether indescribable. I had previously been advised by an old seaman to lash all my trunks and boxes, and I received no damage. But there were a good many who sustained a heavy loss from breakage as well as from awful fright.

Previous to this, scarlet fever had broken out among some of the children. One was the daughter of Mr. and Mrs. Young from Glasgow. I mentioned to Mrs. Young that I had a cure for scarlet fever by wrapping in a wet sheet and that two years ago I applied it with success to three of my own children. She said she had heard of it and would be glad to have it applied. This we did. Three times, and the girl who was 10 years old got better in a day or two.

I spoke to the doctor of the ship about the importance of the wet sheet for scarlet fever but he seemed very much opposed and so I had to keep still. But this did not prevent Mrs. Young and myself from visiting some of those who were affected, and on mentioning how her daughter had been cured, they were willing to have their children treated in the same way. This however had to be done on the sly for fear of the doctor, and in this way we operated on four who all got better in a very little while. But there were several deaths on board from this disease.

We came on the banks of Newfoundland about the 22nd and as it is common, we had some calm and thick fog, but in a day or two we saw lightening and heard thunder. Then it commenced to rain. And then it literally poured in such a way as I had never seen before. It flowed down from the rigging and upper deck in great streams. I equipped myself with my rubber coat and thick boots and with a pail collected great quantities of rain water for my family and others. After this we saw a great many of the fish, porpoises. Our children were much amused to see them sporting in the water and in making their quick gyrations around the ship. We also saw three whales at a distance and saw the blower rising from their nostrils. On the morning of the 28th a woman gave birth to a fine boy. There is a place called the hospital where all such are taken. The captain named the boy Austin Americanus, and he with some others made the parents a present of two guineas.

From this till the 3rd of October the wind was favorable. On the morning of the 2nd the captain said to me that we might now be looking out for a pilot, though he considered we were not yet over 300 miles from New York harbor. That afternoon about 2 o'clock a boat was seen away to the south with a white sail. It soon came nearer so that it was seen to be a pilot boat with the number 19. Our ship slacked sail a little and the boat came alongside. A Yankee stepped on board and took command of the ship. We had some good sailing for a certain time rough. I well recollect that in the morning there was a report that land was seen. I thought that could hardly be the case, but when called to look in a certain direction, sure enough it was land. But on examining my guidebook with its chart, I doubt that we were near the north end of Long Island and the most prominent object we now saw was Montgrue Point. We had been driven this far north by the late storm. The wind being in a southern direction, it took us more than two days to sail tacking out and in from the island till we reached Sandy Hook. As we were thus sailing slowly, a pilot came alongside and the captain invited them to come on board, seeing they had some newspapers, I asked them for one, and on opening, I saw the new[s] that Sabastapool was taken. This I called out and gave a cheer which I knew would offend the captain, as his sympathies were greatly Russian. The two men had luncheon and a bottle of Brandy from the captain. Then they again went with their boat out to sea.

On the morning of the 6th we saw the highlands of New Jersey and Sandy Hook lighthouse. In a little time a large steamer came and took us in tow, and in a little we were between the land of New Jersey and Long Island. The scenery on both sides improved as we advanced till we came to Staten Island. The ground rises undulates: the whole extent is thickly studded with neat villas of a light and airy appearance, clumped and [interspersed] with trees and shrubs of various hues forming altogether a grand panorama of nature and art in combination.

Here the doctor came on board and we passed in review to see that we were all in good health. When we were about 10 yards from the battery, the ship stopped, while a large raft came along and on it was put all the luggage. Here the custom officer had a look to see that we had no excisable goods. A steamer was then attached and the passengers and luggage were then taken alongside the castle gardens. This we found to be a great boon for emigrants, as all outside runners are excluded and everyone needed information as to the place of their destination. Our luggage was all wheeled in and checked. Then we had to pass singly into the interior where we were asked from what country we had come. Then passing on, we were asked to what part of the country we were going—the states or Canada, what business did we follow, and how much money had we brought with us. There were also parties directing our attention to various large maps showing the best and cheapest routes either by steamboat or rail, when and where they started from, and their regular charges. Anyone could remain here for a day or two and get good victuals at a reasonable rate. When they left, their luggage was weighed and the railway or steamboat company came and took it free of expense. The rate of charge was fixed and paid to them, and the emigrant had only to show the Castle Garden Ticket to either steamboat or railroad.

After passing through this ordeal on the Saturday forenoon, I went away up Broadway to see Mr. Gilkerson, who was then foreman in the firm of Bowen and McNames. He took me to the Battery Hotel where my family and I had good lodgings for three days. I had thus some time to call on parties whom I knew, especially Mr. James Buchan and William and John Aitchison, who lived at Brooklyn: and also write letters home to friends, and especially to Mr. Andrew Murray of the *Kelso Chronicle*.

New York looked a large place then, but what an immense change on both it and Brooklyn within the last 30 years! I therefore made arrangements at the Castle Gardens to get my tickets and start for Kalamazoo on Wednesday evening of the 10th. My first ticket was by steam vessel from New York to Albany, with a certain amount of luggage mentioned. We thus started about 6 o'clock in the evening, traveled up the Hudson all night and

arrived about 7 in the morning, at Albany. There we had breakfast and started in the forenoon by rail for Buffalo, for which
we showed our tickets. We thus had a fine view of the Mohawk
Valley, occasionally the Erie Canal and other sights on the line.
But a good part was traveled under night, and we arrived at
Buffalo on the Friday afternoon. Here I had a look round this
city till 6 o'clock when the steamer started along Lake Erie
for Detroit. Here again we showed our tickets and with our
luggage got all on board. We had a night and part of a day sailing on this lake, and in the morning and through the day had
some views to the left of the states of Ohio and Michigan. We
had a better view of the Canadian side as we came nearer to
Detroit.

Here we arrived about 3 in the afternoon and were told that
the Kalamazoo train left at 7 o'clock. I spent a little time looking
round this city. They seemed a good deal engaged in pulling
down old buildings and putting up new. One thing I particularly
noticed was the great number of vessels of all sorts going up and
down the river by the way of Great Lakes. When I went to the
train at 7 o'clock and presented my ticket, they said they could
not take my luggage as this was Saturday evening, but that it
would be sent the beginning of the week. I had therefore to accept
this alternative, and so we took the emigrant cars to Kalamazoo.
We stopped at several places by the way including Marshall,
where we had some good eating. I recollect I went down to where
an old colored lady was cooking, and among other things I
smelled was some fine ham. I made an arrangement with her for
a good plate of this. I brought it up to my family and they ate it
with great relish. They said American ham was far better than
ours at home. I suppose their appetites were getting better after
coming off the sea. As daylight came on, I saw Kalamazoo River.
At that time the banks had a roughish appearance and the rail
fence was a new object in the landscape. Battle Creek seemed
rather a rising place having water power machinery. The morning was calm with a little white frost. And so we passed through

Galesburg [Illinois] and Comstock, and arrived at Kalamazoo about 9 o'clock.

My late brother Andrew met us at the depot and took us up to brother James' house where we had some washing and breakfast. After this, my wife and family went up to Robert Walker's farm at the west end and remained there until I got a house provided. I had come with the expectation of entering on the land which Andrew had wrote to me about some two years before. But I found he had got into some strife in the business which had caused him to give the Rights and Titles of his land into the hands of another party. He told me how his difficulties had come upon him, but that he hoped in a little time to make it all right with me. Brother James, knowing these matters, proposed to let me have a piece of his land opposite the Mountain Home Cemetery, as a nursery. And so I looked out to find a house for my family most convenient to this. The only one I could find was an old one at the corner below the cemetery belonging to Charles Stuart, and the rent he charged was 2 dollars a week. I thought this very high for such a house, but was assured that I could not rent a house any cheaper. Then I had next to look for furniture. James let me have his kitchen stove as they wanted a new one. Then he went round with me to get the other household things, and I found it a fact that to all parties where we went, they were owing a bill for fleshmeat they had been receiving. I thus got all my necessary things collected and so arranged as to commence housekeeping on Saturday 20th of October, 1855.

My luggage meantime had come along to the depot. And when I went to take it, I was quite surprised to find charges on it. I told the agent how I had paid the whole freight and passage at Castle Garden and therefore I refused to pay this charge. He admitted that it might be as I had said, but as they had been charged to pay him, he durst not let them go without payment. I decided to pay under protest and told him I would write the company at Castle Gardens. This I did and received a letter by return post, requesting me to call at the Railway Office and receive the money which I had paid for freight from Detroit to Kalamazoo. This I did and they paid it to me at once, only requiring my signature.

Our first commencement in housekeeping that Saturday evening was not of a cheerful aspect. Through the course of the day, I had got the furniture placed in a certain way and the stove set up, which was something new to me. My wife and family had arrived and had some wondering looking round on the new things. As it began to get dark we had light by the candle and we had also a lamp, but at that time they were a very poor affair and the oil was wretched poor stuff, so that with the black stove and the dim light, the contrast was altogether very great from our open fires and the brilliant gas lights of our house in Kelso. While I felt this, I yet tried to show cheerfulness for my family's sake, and things daily began to brighten up and improve.

5
Life in Michigan and Visits to Scotland

AS I had yet no means for commencing nursery work I studied to make myself useful on the farms, and my first work was taking down and gathering apples. There was a good crop that year, ... the orchard then being young and in good bearing order. Another new kind of work to me was cornhusking, which somewhat brought me into American associations. There was another thing I learned which I had never done before, and that was milking a cow. My brother James in his way of business had always a great many extra cows and cattle on hand. There was one nice red cow among them which he said I could milk and have the use of for my family. I said I had never milked a cow but would try to learn and would get Robert Walker, his man, to show me. So I told Robert and brought up a milking pail. He said he had to learn when he came here and that I would find it quite a simple matter. He then took the pail, went forward and laid his hand gently on the cow and began to milk in quite an easy way, then he got up and I took his place and began milking. But it did not seem to come readily and then the cow began to feel uneasy and moved forward. I tried again and then she made another move. A thought here came over me to give up cowmilking and take a chance of getting milk some other way, but a second thought prevailed and I tried again, found out the proper way to handle the tits and make the milk come freely. And after this, I found it quite a simple matter. We had thus a cow all the 12 years we lived in this west end, and in the course of two or three years some of the boys for the most part did the milking.

It was on the evening of the 10th of November that my youngest son, John was born. My wife soon recovered and for two years had pretty fair health. Isabella and the two oldest boys went to school. On the Sabbath days I went to the Presbyterian Church. The Rev. William Huggins being then the minister. I also joined in the adult Sabbath School Class, and in this way got well acquainted with some of the most intelligent members of the Church. I was also in the way of regularly attending prayer meetings. It was not however till sometime in the spring that I joined this church. My wife was also admitted by our letter.

In the course of the fall and winter of 1855 and 1856, I was employed a good deal with the farm hands in wood chopping. There was a field sown in wheat alongside the Grand Prairie Road where we cut a great many large Oaks, both for firewood and sawlogs. We did a great deal of chopping west of the Lake Shore Road where Vine Street now runs.

I recollect of meeting with a surprise on the last day of that year 1855. I had been up on the farm and on coming down to my house in the evening, some of my family met me on the road and said there was a man from Kelso in the house. This made me wonder, but as I came near I heard loud talking and I was certain it was the voice of Adam Oliver, who I expected was now in Australia. Sure enough, it was the same man. The reason for my wonder at seeing him here was that in the spring he came to me at Kelso to bid me a final goodbye as he was going to Australia where he had a sister. Something had occurred that prevented his going, but induced him to come to Paris in Canada. He had been working and looking around, but not finding things quite to his mind. He had packed up his traps and come with his family to Kalamazoo. His wife and family he said were at the American Hotel. And so I went down town with him and introduced him to brother James, who said he thought he could find him a house in the morning. This he did and I recollect he got him furniture in somewhat the same way as he got mine. He and some of his sons were also engaged in woodchopping on James' farm and also did a good deal of the same work on brother Andrew's land.

The winters of 1855 and 1856 were severe, and I had some experience in cutting and handling ice. Brother James was then in the way of filling a large icehouse which required a good many hands among which were myself and Adam Oliver. We cut from the Mill Pond on Portage Street. I think the ice was from a foot to 15 inches thick.

The ground where I commenced my nursery was ploughed and put in order in the fall. In the course of the winter I sent an order to Stuart and Mein in Kelso for a considerable number of Evergreen trees and ornamental plants, the greater number being the Norway Spruce. My brother James thought at first that I was acting foolishly in planting so many Evergreen trees and that fruit trees would be far more wanted. I said that might have been so when he first came to Kalamazoo, but I could perceive that there were a good many people in the town and country who would like to have their places ornamented, providing such things were properly grown to answer that end. I found on talking with several people about planting Evergreen trees on their grounds. They said they would be willing to do it if they would grow, but that they had once got some and they died. I learned that the Evergreen trees came from agents in the east who were selling fruit trees and sometimes had a few Evergreen. This statement was very conclusive reason to me why Evergreen trees carried about and exposed failed to grow.

The Evergreen trees that I had ordered came in good condition about the beginning of April. I had them all planted out in a proper way, and I scarcely lost a tree. And in the course of the season they grew well as ever I had seen them do in Scotland. I also went into the raising of vegetable plants especially cabbage and tomatoes. I therefore had two or three hotbeds made, [and] did most of the glazing myself. I had a large fine stock of plants in the month of May. The demand for such was greater than I could supply. I transplanted as many of these as I had ground for and sold them all at good prices. All the hotels were good customers and I often left a good supply at my brother's Meat Market, where they were readily sold. Early green peas and sweet corn were also in great demand and brought good prices. I found however, there were some garden products highly esteemed in Scotland which were scarcely known or thought of here. Among these chiefly was celery. That first season of 1856 I transplanted out about 300. It grew well and was of good quality, but then even the hotelkeepers scarcely knew what it was. And it appeared to me at first that I had got a dead stock on my hand. At that time there was an Englishman of the name of Cox, who then kept a small grocery store near to where the post office is now on [Burdick] Street. I showed him some one day and he knew what it was and he said that if I would bring him down a few heads he would talk with people and try to sell it for me. This he did and I kept supplying him with a little as it was wanted. I also took some to my brothers' meat market and they also talked with people and sold some, but it was with some difficulty that myself and the above parties sold the 300 heads.

The next year Mr. Acre of the Burdick House wanted me to bring him a dozen or two every week, then of course the Kalamazoo House had to be supplied in the same way, then certain private families wanted a couple of heads. Before long the thing went on like a house afire, almost everybody wanted it. For nearly ten years I was the principle grower of celery and I made well out by it, as the price at the hotels was never below 50 cents a dozen. At that time it had not been discovered that our Kalamazoo marshes were so well adapted for growing good celery which is now done to a much greater extent than any other place in the United States.

In the course of the next 4 or so years the demand for Evergreen trees began to increase, not only in Kalamazoo but in other towns east and west along the railroad. People had now found out that there was no difficulty in making them grow and so the demand increased in both town and country. There were many

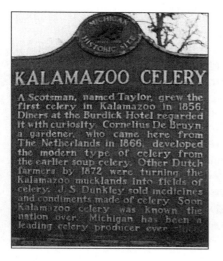

KALAMAZOO CELERY

A Scotsman, named Taylor, grew the first celery in Kalamazoo in 1856. Diners at the Burdick Hotel regarded it with curiosity. Cornelius De Bruyn, a gardener, who came here from The Netherlands in 1866, developed the modern type of celery from the earlier soup celery. Other Dutch farmers by 1872 were turning the Kalamazoo mucklands into fields of celery. J S Dunkley sold medicines and condiments made of celery. Soon Kalamazoo celery was known the nation over. Michigan has been a leading celery producer ever since.

9. Michigan State plaque on site of historic interest noting George Taylor's role in introducing the cultivation of celery to Kalamazoo.

SOURCE: JIM HIGGINS

people at that time who made some great mistakes in planting these Evergreen trees so near the front of their houses. They looked very well for a few years, but as they grew larger, many of them had to be cut down. I was thus in the first place making some money while the people on their part were learning something by experience.

* * *

It was about this time that I introduced a form of planting Evergreen trees as a hedge, more especially the Norway Spruce. The first which I sold for this purpose was on the north side of the town to Mr. Humphry on the Gull Road. He had just got his large new house finished and the ground leveled round about. He called on me to see about getting some Evergreens for his place, and he mentioned that some person had advised him to plant a row of the Norway Spruce for a hedge. I told him to plant them 2 ½ feet apart. I sold him 200 good bushy plants 18 inches high for 15 cents each. The hedge was well tended and trim and became the admiration of every one that passed along the road: an advertisement from what I received a great benefit.

As the spring came round, I put advertisements in our local papers, and by this means I had a great deal of custom from the farmers in the county. I had also some agents at Battle Creek, Marshall, and Jackson. The same also on the western line, such as Dowag[i]ac and Niles, and for some time I also sent a good many to an agent in Chicago. The grounds of the Mountain Home Cemetery were laid out with regular drives about this time and I supplied the company with 100 dollars for decoration.

It was in the winter of 1857 that I commenced a large stock of young Apple trees by root grafting. This is a Yankee invention, and here I found its superiority to what was our practice in Scotland. They succeeded well and I soon found customers from the farmers around.

Some of the people in Kalamazoo were now beginning to acquire a taste for flowers and ornamental plants. I had got with some of my nursery orders from Stuart and Mein, two or three dozen of the finest varieties of Herbaceous plants, as well as some of the finest Hybrid Perpetual Roses. I recollect that in one of these import[at]ions they sent me a few seeds of the *Delphinium Formosum*. This was the first year that this new variety was offered to the public and it came out with great praise, as it had been awarded the first prize at the Royal Horticultural Society of London, the last years as the finest new variety of Herbaceous plants. I think I started these seeds in the Hotbed and planted them out carefully. They grew freely and flowered profusely in the months of July and August. In September I noticed a good many seed pods on the stalks that had flowered. I carefully gathered them. It so happened that the Michigan State Fair was held in Detroit that year and I thought I would go and see it. And as there were a good many of the Delphiniums coming into the second blood, I cut a fine large bouquet and took it with me, and also a good package of the seed I had gathered. I had this bouquet of Delphiniums shown off in a conspicuous place, and it soon attracted a large crowd of wondering ladies. Of course I had to tell the name and especially that this was the flower that received the highest prize at the Royal Horticultural Society of London. I sold a dozen seeds for 25 cents, altogether about 12 dollars worth.

This good success in Detroit led me to try the same scheme in another direction. This occurred in about 3 weeks later at Chicago where the Illinois State Fair was held. I had never been to Chicago before and was therefore the more encouraged to go. And so I took a bouquet of the same as I did at Detroit and showed it off, talked with the ladies and sold a large amount.

There was about half an acre of ground round about my old house and it was here where I cultivated my flower garden. Here I showed such a collection of fine things as altogether new to the place. Hybrid Perpetual Roses were one of these, and I was in the way of propagating a large stock both by budding and layering. The fine display attracted a great many visitors, certain of the ladies ordered freely and instructed me to collect the bill from their husbands. In one or two cases I was plainly told that if their wives ordered any more this way they would not settle the bill. Of Dahlias and Hollyhocks I had also the finest collection and strangers from other towns and the country were frequent visitors. All my gardening operations for the first 3 or 4 years were done with the aid of Hotbeds. ... There was another party who had commenced a greenhouse in town, and was in the way of selling a good many bedding and houseplants. This man's name was Watkins and was from New York, and knew the business well; but he often indulged in drinking habits and got into debt with a great many till he was obliged to sell out. This he proposed to me at a cheap rate, and so I bought his greenhouse and stock of plants, which I had moved up at once to my own garden grounds. This I think was in the fall of 1859.

My wife's health through the course of this last year had been very poor, and I had called in the skill of two of our best physicians, Mottrem and Pratt, but she seemed only to get weaker and died about the end of September of that year. Her disease no doubt was one of the many forms of Consumption. My oldest daughter, Isabella, took charge of our housekeeping, and with the advice of some of our good neighbors kept all things in good order.

Our nursery business seemed still to increase. My brother had cleared out about two acres to the south of the nursery which he had bought to square up his land. This also was appropriated by me for the growing of trees and vegetables, as for this I also found the demand increasing. All this with the greenhouse greatly increased our amount of work, but my boys were now coming to be of great help, not only of garden work, but also for marketing.

It was about this time that I was induced to purchase two acres adjacent from Mr. Benedict, our neighbor on the College Addition. This I paid by so much down and the rest in the course of two years. This lot was mostly planted with Apple and Peach trees and was now in good bearing order. I was also in the way of cultivating a good many strawberries and other vegetables among the fruit trees. This lot I still hold and have been offering it for sale for the last three years.

For the first two or three years after I came to this country, I had some scruples in taking out my papers as an American citizen. I had always protested against slavery and it appeared to me that the government was in some way identified with it. But I could perceive that a conflict was coming on, and therefore I thought I would become a citizen and fight the battle with the Antislavery party. I found even in Kalamazoo a good many though proud of being American citizens, and democrats were yet haters of the nigger and advocates of slavery. I even found that certain parties belonging to our churches and teachers in our Sabbath Schools were holding that slavery was a divine institution and were ready to prove it from the Bible authority. Of this I had a noted instance in our own Presbyterian Sabbath School. I was in the adult class, and that portion of the Scripture came up for our lesson in Ephesians 6th chapter, 5th verse where the Apostle enjoins servants to be obedient to their master with fear and trembling and singleness of heart. I think there were about 8 or 10 who were regular members in this class, and as near as I could estimate, there were 3 or 4 Democrats and other Republican and Abolitionists. The great question insisted on by the Democratic party was that the text of this lesson enjoined slavery and that in the books of Moses there were certain injunctions given to the Israelites in their buying and selling of slaves. For 6 Sabbaths we debated the matter, and considerable numbers came round to hear this question of the hour discussed. After all the parties had given their reasons for and against, I directed the class to look at this question in the light of the divine progression, as the scope of the Bible and the Plan of Salvation more especially as it was brought out in the teachings of the Savior and the Apostles as recorded in the New Testament Scriptures. To give an instance of this, I directed the class to look at some of the imperative laws of Moses, and what would be the effect upon us if we should put these same divine laws into effect in our state of Michigan. For instance, a son that was rebellious and disobedient to his parents was to be stoned to death, the same for an open violation of the Sabbath and certain others of the same sort. We are not now under a Theocrasy but under the dispensation of the New Testament, and the grand Golden Rules of the great Master which at once settles this whole question: "Whatsoever ye would that men should do to you, do ye even so to them." This brought our discussion to a termination, and the end of the Civil War four years afterwards confirmed it.

Previous to and all through the time of the War, our money system was in a very unsettled condition. The banks of the various states having issued bills, many of these had become depreciated and some were nearly worthless. For sometime no person durst take a bill till looking into a book of record. On many of them there was a discount of ten, twenty, and thirty percent. This Civil War created a great excitement all over the country, and a great deal of trouble and distress to those who were subject to the draft as soldiers. It was a serious time with all right thinking people, and some of us as church members [had] frequent meetings for prayer that the Lord would guide and direct our rulers and that our success in this great conflict might be equal to the justice of our cause, and I am happy to think that these prayers were fully answered.

In the summer of 1862 I thought I would like to run across and see the Old Country once more. My boys being certain that they could manage the business with a little assistance in my absence. I therefore started from Kalamazoo with the early train to Detroit. Spent the day seeing some Scotch friends, started at 6 o'clock by rail to Albany, checking my trunk to that place. As I had a great desire to see Niagara Falls, I spoke to the conductor about this, and he gave me a layover ticket. Our train arrived there in the morning about 5 o'clock. I went out and went down to the end of the bridge. The river here being narrow begins to move quickly and I was induced to walk down for about half a mile and see the whirlpool. After looking at this wonderful [gulf] and the scenery around it, I came up again to the end of the bridge, and seeing an eating house I went up in and had a good plain breakfast. I found the lady that kept this very intelligent, and mentioned that I was now going up to the Falls, [and] she gave me some advice to take care of sharpers [thieves]. She said there is some near by, pointing at some Hackmen with carriages. I thanked her, but I thought I could clear my way.

No sooner had I shown myself then the Hackmen were at me in full mouth, most persistent to take me up to the Falls. I allowed them to talk some time and then calmly told them that I was going to have the pleasure of walking and saving my money. I then slowly went up, often stopping and looking at the River and the steep rugged banks by the way. The view of the great Falls from this Canadian side as you draw near is truly grand, as you stand a great measure in front of them. I went up where there was a large Inn and some interesting sights, but I did not spend any money. In my observations I had seen a small boat passing back and forward, a little below the falls. As it was drawing near, I went down and found their charge was 15 cents for taking me across. This I paid and thought it well spent, as the view of the Falls and the water still whirling and surging around was an extra sight.

On arriving at the foot of the bank I found two ways of ascending. One was by an elevator and the other by a winding staircase. I chose the latter, where I could rest and look around at the grand scenery. On coming to the top, I found myself a little to the right of the American Fall. After looking over this grand precipice I walked up a little way, where were several large hotels, but I did not patronize any of them. Then I had to cross a bridge or bridges to Goat Island which charge I think was 25 cents. I then went down to the precipices and had a look into the great gorge of the Horseshoe Fall which was awfully grand. As I stood on the verge looking over I thought if any demon or spirit had the power, how easily they could push me over, but then that Scripture came to my mind, "He shall give his Angels charge concerning thee." Then I felt calm and confident. I walked round this Island, saw the rapids and some other fine sights. I sat down in a retired place and had about an hours sleep. Then there was a calm eddy in the stream where I took a bath. I then came back the same way looking on the sights around, and then came slowly down the banks to the village and station at the end of the bridge. I had been here eating in a cheap way, and the train not starting for Albany till after 6 o'clock, I had a walk down and saw the whirlpool from this American side.

I found an intelligent man at the station who was also going to Albany and from there to New York by steamboat as I intended. He had traveled this same way before and could therefore give me the names of the places. We arrived at Albany about 6 o'clock in the morning. This was the first time I had experienced the great benefit of our check system. I had told my friend that I expected my trunk here. Just as we stepped from the cars, a man was calling for baggage for the boat. I gave him my check and was assured my trunk would be at the boat when it leaves at 9. My friend and I had a walk and saw the capitol, had breakfast, and went down to the boat. It was a pleasant day and we had a fine view of all the noted places on each side of the River. This was all new to me, as when I came up seven years ago, it was under night.

*   *   *

We arrived at the wharf at New York about 5 o'clock, and my friend took me to a good hotel where he had stopped before, so passed a good night, and after breakfast went down to the Steamship Office No. 9 Broadway to secure a Passage Ticket. As I came near the place I was surprised to see a large crowd around the office. On inquiring, I was told that they wanted to secure passage to the Old Country and could not obtain it. I then made an effort to get into the office and find the reason why a Passage Ticket could not be obtained. After some difficulty I got word with one of the clerks who said they had got a dispatch from Washington this morning forbidding selling tickets to men without civic authority. The reason being that they wanted to escape the Draft.

A thought here struck me that I would go direct to the shipping office at the dock and hear what they had to say. I went up Broadway and down one of the streets to the left, where the office was. As I went in there I saw two or three men sitting with their feet up doing little or nothing. I asked if I could have a Steerage Passage to Liverpool and back in the course of three months. They said I could or even to London if I wished. I then asked what a round ticket would be from London and was told 75 dollars. I said I would take it, but that I had not got my Bank Check cashed yet, but would pay them 10 dollars now as security till I got my money at Wall Street.

All right, they said, and so I went and got my check cashed at a discount then of 11 percent. On coming back to the office they said, "Why we did not know when you were here that an order had come to this company from Washington not to sell any tickets to men without an order from the mayor of the city." "Well," I said, "Gentlemen, I could have told you that, but as you know I'm not running away to escape the draft, I shall now pay you the balance of my passage money and you can write me out a ticket as a receipt." They gave a laugh and said I had rather come smart over them. On Saturday forenoon there was a good deal of trouble with the civic authorities, but about noon the company had a dispatch that all who had taken passages were allowed to go. This vacillating of the authorities at Washington caused a delay of our ships sailing till 5 o'clock in the afternoon. There was a great deal of trouble and confusion. I got an appointment in a berth which held 8 persons. There were 6 Irish men and 1 Englishman and myself. These men had been in this country for some time and were much more clean and respectable in appearance than as I had seen them coming from Ireland.

The weather was favorable for the first four days and about that time our ship touched at Cape Race and took in the last news of the war. Our rations were pretty good and I got along first rate with my Irish neighbors in the berth. Our vessel had about 600 on board, and as the weather was pretty good we spent a good deal of our time on deck. I got acquainted with some of the cabin passengers and had a good time with them. One was a Presbyterian minister of Delhi in York State who was well acquainted with our cousins, the Mables. We had religious services on board once or twice. I think we saw land about the 19th, touched at the harbor of Queenston. As we were entering, a small boat came alongside for mail with the last news from America which was no doubt sent over the telegraph wires to Ireland and Great Britain. The majority of our passengers went out here.

I think we came into the harbor of Liverpool on the forenoon of the 21st. Before leaving the ship, our trunks and parcels had to be examined by the Excise Officers. Tobacco being one of the things they looked for, I saw several packages taken. We spent two or three hours in the city and took the train for Carlisle about 2 o'clock. The minister from Delhi and other Scotchmen were with us. As soon as the train came to Carlisle, I had to secure another ticket by the Midland line to Newto[w]n Roxburgh County. Then I had to push about among the throng of people, get out my trunk, and have a label to Newton put on it. Here again I found the advantages of our American Check system. I again got on board the train and along the new road that had been made since I left. We touched at Hawick, where my friends left me and arrived at Newton about 8 o'clock. Here I had a good rest at the hotel, rose early in the morning, and went down to St. Boswells and saw the old man, Brotherstone, and delivered him a present of money from his son Andrew in America.

* * *

From that village I came down a steep bank to the Tweed, and running forward I plunged my hands into her limpid water, as having once more met with an old friend. Here Dryburgh with its old Abb[e]y lies close on the other side, where the bones of the great Minstrel, Sir Walter Scott, rest. I came up the side of the river to the hotel where I had breakfast and awaited the train for Roxburgh at 9. The train from Edinburgh took us on to Roxburgh, where there is a connection to Jedburgh. Seven years ago this road was just being talked about. So I purchased a ticket and had the pleasure of riding over the old ground on the cars, where I had so often walked it. The station I found was at the Bongate Bridge. After passing the tollgate, my eye caught the Cottage House, where my mother lived when I left seven years before. She was not there now, but had passed to the Higher Mansion about a year before.

I went up the Bongate Road across the [Goosepool] Bridge and up through the old town, where I had walked so often through the Market Place, and then along the Rampart by the side of the graveyard and the old Abb[e]y. Then across the Jed and up round by the Free Church. Just as I made the town here, my sister Agnes saw me. When I received a most hearty welcome.

My sister Margaret Telfer was living just a little way off and we were soon all together.

After dinner I went away through the park to the Hartrigge Garden to see my brother John, where I had another cordial reception. I found the garden had greatly improved since I left. He had some of the finest strawberries. This was the more of a wonder to me as ours in America were all over two months before. This variety I think was called the Elton Pine. There was another thing in the garden with which I was much gratified, that was some very fine large peaches. These trees had come from our Kelso nursery and being finely trained on the wall, the fruit was much larger than any I had ever seen in this country. I also visited our friends at Bonjedward and Jane Wheelance [Whellans?] at Grahamslaw.

When at Kelso I stopped with my old friend Robert Rutherford. Then I had to see all the gentlemen gardeners and many others in town and neighborhood. Sometime in September I was induced to make a trip to Ireland, and this was with my brother-in-law, William Huggan. He was in the way of doing a good deal of Millwright business in that country, and his daughter Janet was married to a Mr. Laing, who was then living in Dublin.

We went by the way of Edinburgh and there saw my sister Mary and her son, Andrew Stevenson. Then to Glasgow and took the steamer at night which sails for Dublin. The vessel was a good deal crowded and my hand satchel, which was laid aside among some others, was stolen. Several more of the passengers raised the alarm that they also lost certain things. This led to the captain and officers to make a general investigation. Two men were found who had certain things that were identified by those who had lost them. But my satchel with shirts, razors, and other things was never seen. I think there was a fault with this vessel in not having a place to check all such things.

We soon found a Mr. and Mrs. Lain[g] who lived alongside of the [Phoenix] Park near the banks of the Liffey. One of the first things that strikes a stranger in this city is their jaunting cars with the seats on every side, the long way, instead of across. I found I could ride all over the city in this way at a moderate charge. I spent about a week in this city. There are some fine government buildings and also some shops in the central parts; but on the outsides, a great many poor shops and other wretched buildings. Any person of genteel appearance going along is constantly accosted with beggars. One of the finest things about that city is the Phoenix Park, both for size and variety. It is said that with the Vice Regal grounds and gardens there is altogether about twenty-two hundred acres. I saw a great many deer, sheep, and goats. There are fine carriage drives all round and through it. I called several times at the Vice Regal Gardens and got intimate with the head gardener who was a Scotchman. These gardens and grounds are kept in fine order.

* * *

This city has a fine museum which I visited once or twice. Nearby is the [Glasnevin] Cemetery. Any person that would want to know something about Catholicism, its religious ties and ceremonies should visit such a place. This burial ground seemed a good deal crowded with a good many plain, upright grave stones. I noticed that a great many of these, after mentioning the name of the deceased[,] had also requested friends to pray for the soul of the party whose name was mentioned.

I noticed that when a funeral procession came along, they had to wait on a large open space outside the gate till the priest and some other church officials came and escorted the funeral to the grave. Here a good deal of ceremonials had to be gone through, among which was the sprinkling with Holy Water. At one time I was standing so near I felt a small squirt of it but it seemed to have no effect on me for good or evil, but I felt a deep sorrow for the poor blind deluded people.

We left Dublin by rail for Belfast. This was in the early part of the day, which gave us a fine opportunity of seeing the country.

But what a contrast in traveling through the same space in either Scotland or England. Here we saw hundreds of small holdings with wretched buildings and poor cultivation. This verified to me what I had heard from some of the Irishmen who came over to the Harvest in Scotland, many of which were farmers of the lands I now saw. I noticed however, that as we came nearer Belfast, the farming of the land was greatly improved, larger, and better managed. Here a great deal of Flax is cultivated for Linen Manufacture. I was told that a great many of the people here are Protestant.

We reached Belfast about 4 o'clock and found the steamboat to Greenock sailed about six. Before sailing, my friend, Huggan pointed my attention to a certain object as it suspended on a high pinnacle, asking if I knew what it meant. I did not and was told that it was a storm signal. He did not want to go. We started out in a fair way, but sure enough about 9 o'clock the wind began to blow and Huggan's fear began with symptoms of sea sickness. He then engaged a berth where he could lie down. But the wind still increased and his sickness increased with severe vomiting. I once or twice looked in on him, when he gave me a wicked agonizing look. I went down to the hold of the vessel where I witnessed an awful scene of sickness and throwing and soon left for the deck. I now felt a little sickness coming over myself and engaged a berth for a small fee from a seaman. I had now a little spell of throwing which at once gave me [relief]. When it got calmer I went and saw Huggan. He had now got over his sickness and he seemed to be more pleased when I told him what I saw in the hold. He said he would now like to go and see that place, so I led the way. But when we got to the top of the gangway there were a number of men pulling with ropes to extricate a steer that had fallen into the hatchway. Afterwards we went down and found the people in an awful fright. Huggan now seemed more pleased when he saw so many others worse than himself.

We then got washed and brushed up a little, had a nice view of the banks of the Clyde, and when we came to Glasgow, had some appetite for breakfast. We then came home by the way of Edinburgh to Jedburgh.

Having a free passage ticket from Liverpool to London, I had to go there and get it certified. I therefore took the railroad to Carlisle and from the seaport near there by steamer to Liverpool. We started at night in good order, but the wind soon rose to a perfect gale worse than from Belfast. I had a severe spell of sea sickness but got over it and had a rest of two or three hours on the vessel in the harbor. I then got my ticket to London and started with the morning train. By a mistake I boarded the express and had the pleasure of a quick trip to London. I went direct down to Cheapside and from there to Bow Lane where I lodged in 1851. The same lady recognized me again and said she could give me lodgings. I then had dinner and a walk down to the London Bridge.

The World's Exposition of 1862 was now being held in London and the city was thronged with strangers. The buildings for this were in the Kensington Gardens and were not light and elegant as the Crystal Palace of 1851. There were a great many wonderful things exhibited. Owing to the Civil War, the American display was more limited than would otherwise have been. But the Crystal Palace at Sydenham was in fine running order, and the fine display on the outside ground there with the many floral shades and figures of the new ribbon system were the admiration of every visitor. I kept looking round London for a few days. Once I took an excursion down the Thames to Sheerness and saw some of the ship building operations. I visited Woolwich and saw some of the great guns and a great many other military tactics. Another day I took a railroad excursion to Bristol. I never had been on the west side of the island before. I wanted to see George Muller[']s Orphan Institution, of which I had read. The train reached Bristol in the afternoon, and I could see at a distance the various buildings of the asylum on the high grounds of Ashley Down. They are nearly a mile from the centre of the city. As I drew nearer I met large companies of boys walking with their attendants. I found the buildings fitted up with economy and utility. I had some conversation with some of the officials. I called at the office and registered my name, and as I was a stranger in the city, they gave me the address of a Christian family where I would find cheap and comfortable lodgings.

It was now beginning to get dark and on asking for the street and the place where I intended to lodge and then going in that direction, I was accosted by a well dressed lady who said she would take me to good lodgings. I declined her offer as I had already made an engagement. She then showed her true character and took certain liberties, the same as I had sometimes experienced in Edinburgh in my early days. I soon found the place to which I had been directed and had a very pleasant and comfortable lodgings. I took the train in the morning and arrived at London in the afternoon.

The fame of Mr. Spurgeon as a preacher had now become well known, and one Sabbath I found my way to the Tabernacle. In the afternoon I went to the Rowland Hill Chapel to see and hear my old friend Rev. Newman Hall. That large house was also filled to full extent. I waited on him in the vestry after service and he was very happy to meet me again.

I found that the Civil War created a cotton famine, and I saw thousands of workmen going about idle, awaiting with anxiety the news of every steamer that touched Queenston. I found it to be much the same in London, where the news of the morning and evening papers were awaited with anxiety. I well recollect one morning while sitting at breakfast I noticed the landlady come in from the door with the *London Times* in her hand, and as I looked and gave a signal, she passed the paper to me. On opening it I at once saw in large heading, "President Lincoln Proclamation to Free the Slave."

I at once gave a hurrah for Lincoln and Liberty to the slaves. This called out some comment by various parties at the table, some saying that it could not be done and would end in a blast of wind. I found the general impression was that the Northern

States should divide with the South and let them retain their slaves.

I came back to Scotland by the Eastern line [via] York and Newcastle. I here made a call on George Taylor and his wife, a cousin of mine, who kept a furniture store. I spent a night with them and then came by way of Berwick to Kelso. Brother Alexander was then Farm Steward at Burnfoot where I stopped a few days, calling on some of my old acquaintances about Morebattle. I made a selection of Nursery Stock to take home with me. Among some of the new things were 250 European Linden, the first I suppose that ever came to Michigan, and also a few cuttings of the Black Italian Poplar. I have often the pleasure of looking at many of the fine specimens now growing round Kalamazoo.

I had spoken to Jane Wheelence [Whellans?] about going to Kalamazoo with me, signifying that I needed a person of her experience both to look after myself and family. After thinking over the matter she thought she would go. She had a good situation as housekeeper at Grahamslaw, but there was no certainty of this. I said I thought it might be better not to enter into a marriage relationship until we get home to Kalamazoo. She then gave up her situation and made the necessary arrangement to leave for America. After seeing all the friends, we started about the beginning of November for Liverpool. My passage of course was previously secured, and so we took the first of the companies vessels that sailed for New York. We were taken out of the harbor by a tug and then made our way for Queenston. We remained in the harbor for two hours and took a great many passengers. Among these were several that came over with me in the month of August. They said they found that America was the best country for a working man.

We had some pretty rough weather, heaving the ship and sometimes washing over the deck. Jane Wheelence [Whellans?] stood the trip well. She got a good berth with several respectable ladies. I also got acquainted with some intelligent gentlemen where we met together after the greater part had retired and discussed various matters. I met a man of the name of Brewster, son of Sir David Brewster of Jedburgh. Once when we were alone, he told me he had been in the Southern States for some time, but when the war broke out he did not wish to engage in hostilities. But he thought there was a chance to make something by running the blockade, and so with certain other parties, made one fortunate hit, but the next time were caught and kept prisoners for some time. Then after being liberated he took passage to England and when in Liverpool, he got acquainted with certain parties on this vessel who secured him this passage to New York. He seemed to be quite familiar with that city and told of a lodging house at the foot of Chambers Street where I could order anything I wanted and have a separate lodging bill. I went to this place when we landed and found cheap and good accommodations. It was from this Mr. Brewster that I first heard of the *Alabama*. He said our ship had 5,000 stand of arms aboard and he hoped that vessel would come and take them. I said I hoped we would escape, more especially as I had a good many young trees and plants which I would be sorry to lose. We however got into port without seeing the *Alabama*, and after passing through the Castle Gardens, I next went to get my box of trees through the custom house. This I found was no easy business. I had heard that there was a great deal of roguery connected with this Institution and I now had proof and experience. I think I went before half a dozen different officials who had certain questions to ask. Then I had to sign certain papers and pay certain charges. One paper required me to go before an appraiser to ascertain a value to reach the office of this party. I had to walk about a mile. I was heartily sick of this business and was glad when I got my box on the train.

We took our railroad passage by the New York Southern by way of Elmira [New York], where we stopped two hours for a connection. Then we came to Rochester, where we stopped all night and took the train in the morning to Niagara Falls. We stopped at one of the inns there, went to church in the forenoon, and after took a walk up and saw all round the Falls. In the evening we again attended church and heard an excellent sermon.

The next morning we started for Detroit, and I was not a little surprised to find on the train my brother James. He had been east with a car load of sheep and was on his way home. I also met on this train our great Michigan senator, Macharia Chandler. Brother James introduced me as having been making a visit to our English neighbors. This brought him out pretty strong upon the way England had been acting toward our government lately, but he was certain we would yet get about with her for action. I told him that she was suffering a good deal on our account. This brought out the sentiment which I had expressed that England was one of the chief agents that nourished and upheld slavery in this country. He seemed confident we would put down the South and slavery.

We arrived at Kalamazoo in the morning and had a happy reception from our family. I found that Andrew and the boys had managed our business affairs pretty well, and our household affairs were also greatly improved by the assistance of cousin Jane Whillence [Whellans?].

We had arranged to go through the forms of marriage on the 1st of January 1863. Dr. Stone who was then our neighbor, performing that ceremony. All that spring and summer everything went on pleasant and agreeable till the 24th of August, when my oldest son, Andrew, lost his life by accidental drowning in one of our small lakes. He had been downtown as usual in the forenoon marketing our vegetables, and while at dinner he said that he would like if I could spare him time to go out to the Twin Lakes with his gun this afternoon, where there was some good duck shooting. I said as he had been in the way of working so well, that I would have no objection. He then started, accompanied with his younger brother James. And after going to the lake he shot a duck which fell a little way in the lake. There being no means of getting it out. He thought as he was a good swimmer, he would go in for it. Thus far all seemed right, but there was one thing he had not taken into calculation, that in this part of the lake there was a great growth of aquatic plants, whose roots and stems are below the water forming a sort of tangled network. It was among this hidden trap that he so entangled himself he could not extricate himself, and so he sank and was drowned before any means of rescue could be obtained. The body was brought home in a light wagon by one of the neighboring farmers, and it was a sad shock to me and the rest of the family. He had particularly distinguished himself at school as a fine scholar and was of a most kind, loving, and obliging disposition. There was something altogether different in him from any of the family, and the way and manner of his death had always seemed to me a most wonderful providence. It may possibly be fully disclosed to me in a future life.

But there was another sad affliction which [be]fell me shortly after this. The time had come for my wife to give birth to a child and her illness was of a protracted nature. The child was a large fine boy, but by the very severe labor, was strangled in Life's Porch. We had some slight hope at first that she might recover, but on the second day a sort of stup[o]r came over her and she passed away in a most pleasant manner with a smile on her countenance.

My daughter Isabella had again to resume our housekeeping and continued so till Violet was able for this. For a year or two I was still doing a good business in the nursery, both in evergreens and fruit trees. About this time I was induced to purchase a piece of land from Mr. Sabin Nicols on Grand Prairie. There was 20 acres with no buildings but all well fenced. The price I think was 1,500 dollars. I paid a part of this down and the remainder in the course of three years. On the greater part of this land, I grew farm crops but I also grew a good deal of sweet corn, cabbage, turnips, and celery. I now kept one horse and wagon, but had most of my plowing done by the farmers.

The war was still going on and the tendency was to greatly derange business and all money matters. But it seemed to me truly wonderful how so many men left their homes and exposed themselves to all the hardships of the camps and the dangerous conflict on the battlefield. I noticed that all the time this great conflict was going on, the Democratic Party were often in the way of getting up meetings and sometimes with street parades and bearing certain emblems caricaturing the acts of President Lincoln and the Republican Party. It seemed that while they had a strong desire to maintain our National Independence, they had at the same time an utter abhorrence of the nigger. And in the second campaign when Lincoln was re-elected, one of the planks in their platform was that the "War had been a failure". I think that as we look back upon the past, the Democratic Party had a most une[n]viable record.

It was a great and happy achievement for this country when the War was brought to a termination, but just upon this, the Nation and World was shocked by the assassination of President Lincoln.

My brother Andrew had now for some time given up his store in town and was living on his farm. He kept a number of cows and went into the milk business for two or three years. He had also sold off several lots to parties for building on both along the Alcott Street and also at the Parkhouse on Portage. He had also made a [plot] of lots alongside where Reid Street is now opened. In talking with him one day, he mentioned that he had now made arrangements with Mr. Breese to sell building lots, and that if I would come over and look around this place I could now get whatever land I might require for a nursery. I said it would certainly be more satisfactory for me to have a larger nursery and also a place which I could call my own. A day was then appointed. This was some time in the month of August 1866. When I came over I met him at the road near his house. We then started to walk westward where Reid Street now runs toward the Mill race. As we went along, I mentioned that this [plot] of ground to the left which was nice and level was just right for a nursery. We then came to the race and walked up the side for a certain distance, when I stopped and said that ten acres from here to the Portage Road would be as much as I would take to make me a good nursery. He then mentioned that I should have had this land when I came here, had not a certain circumstance prevented, but he would now make it all right with me. Now he said we will take a walk up as far as the large oak tree at the corner of the fence. When there he said now from this along the fence to Portage Road would make you a most complete nursery. This land is now worth 250 dollars per acre and I now propose that you can have the whole agreeing to pay me at your convenience 800 dollars. I then said I would agree to that proposal. He then mentioned that Mr. Breese had been a good friend in helping him out of his troubles and that he would like to show him all the gratitude he could, and if I would just do him the favor to make a mortgage deal of this land to Mr. Breese, he would see that it should never come against me. In this friendly way, without thinking over the matter, I signed that Mortgage to Mr. Breese merely as a matter of form.

But I found to my cost afterwards that I had made a sad mistake, for it so happened that only six months after this, my brother died suddenly while traveling in the South, and so the mortgage came against me and also the balance of the 800 dollars to his widow, which she was not slow in exacting. I commenced building a new house and barn the next year, and through the course of the winter had the stone drawn for building the cellar and foundation. We had fixed on the site of the house where my brother had planted an orchard a few years before. I can well recollect our first beginning with a sleigh load of stones which my son James and I brought from the west end of Grand Prairie. The only entrance from the road then was by the upper gate betwixt two oak trees. Then we had to pass down a hollow where the snow was deep and it was a very hard pull for the horses. This with the present surroundings had rather a hard look for a beginning, but we still continued drawing till we had a large pile. We also drew a good deal of our lumber from a yard near to where the South Haven Road now runs, about 16 miles from Kalamazoo.

That summer of 1867 was an extra busy one with both gardening and house building. I was fortunate in having sold my farm lot on Grand Prairie the previous year at a pretty fair price. I had now however a large outlay of money both for materials and wages. George Turned [Turner?], a new neighbor, was the builder of the house and barn. The whole work with the plastering was finished so that I was able to enter and occupy it about the middle of November. I mind it was a cold afternoon and I had a good deal of trouble in fitting up the stove pipes. I thus left the old house on the west end where I had spent my first 12 years in Kalamazoo, and in the course of that time I had paid Charles Stuart for house rent with the little garden attached the sum of 1,250 dollars. I found also a good deal of trouble and labor in removing my nursery stock. Those that were small were not such a difficult matter, but I had some large stock which took me a couple of years to clear out. On the new ground I put in a great many of the different sorts of shade trees and found a good sale for them. Then I set about grading and leveling round the house planned for a drive in, also a grass lawn and flower borders and shrubbery, Evergreen trees, so planted and disposed as to have a harmonious effect. I also planted certain varieties of hedge along the roadside, consisting of Beech, Barberry, and Norway Spruce. In this last I made an experiment which was successful. I planted the hedge between the first and second growth. Every tree grew and there were over 150. This hedge is cut every season in the month of August. It is a model from which a great many other have been sold.

There was now a good deal of fencing needed all round the place. There was one especially needed from the race to Portage Street, forming the south line where Reid Street was to run. All the fencing and labor cost a good deal of money.

The second year after I came to this place, I was induced to enter into a certain speculation which turned out anything but profitable. My late brother's widow still held the land and she proposed to let me have the three fields to the south of the nursery nearly 40 acres at a certain yearly rental. I agreed to this for one year, and had it plowed and planted with potatoes and corn. I had a good crop of both but it cost me a good deal for hired labor, and then I had to pit and store a great quantity of the potatoes. These being in large deep pits, a good many of them rotted, so that altogether I lost several hundred dollars by this engagement.

The next year Mrs. Taylor, my late brother's widow, was so fortunate to sell the farm to three parties: Reid, Cobb, and Wells for the sum of $25,000. As a matter of justice and equity, the mortgage which I had signed at the request and promise of my late brother should now have been cancelled, but I never mentioned the circumstances thinking that as I had done so well in my business hitherto I would soon be able to meet this or that a wealthy man li[k]e Mr. Breese would ever enforce by law such an unjust claim. But I learned afterwards that the laws of God and the laws of Michigan can be made to operate in a very different way. I think I paid on this mortgage at different times the sum of $1,500.00, besides the $800 to my brother and his widow.

My oldest daughter Isabella was now teaching school, and my youngest daughter Violet was acting as housekeeper. I think about this time my son James attended Business College a season or two, and George and John rendered help to me in the Nursery and vegetable department. In the winter we were kept busy in drawing manure from various parts in town. This now cost some money being very different from when I first came, when I could get all I wanted for the drawing away.

As I had been relying on my daughter for my housekeeping for the last seven years and had not security how long this might continue, I thought it might be well to look out for one upon whom I might permanently rely, and so I got acquainted with my present wife, Susan Carter, who for a good many years I had known as an assistant housekeeper with Mrs. Henry Breese. So the preliminary arrangements being made, we were married at their house in Kalamazoo on the 20th of January 1870.

We took the evening train that night to Three Rivers, came

back the next evening to Schoolcraft, where we spent two or three days with friends and acquaintances, and then settled down at our home in Kalamazoo.

Mrs. Henry Breese had by a former marriage two sons and a daughter. The sons had gone out some years previous to California and had there taken up farms. One of the youngest of those sons, Romulo E. Bangs, made a visit to his friends about this time, and so a marriage was arranged with my daughter Isabella, which took place at our house a few months after in the same year 1870. They then returned to their home farm which is near Modesto, Stanislaw County.

I do not recollect of any particular incident occurring till the Fall of 1871 when I thought I would make a trip to the west and southward, where I had never been before. I therefore started for Chicago on an early morning train, where I landed at that city about 8 o'clock. My first business here was to call upon a man who had been in the way for some years of having a considerable number of Evergreen trees for the decoration of the suburbs of the city. He lived on Division Street and I found him and got a settlement for a bill of about one hundred dollars. I intended to go to St. Louis and [as] the evening train did not start till 9, I spent the day in looking round the city where great building and improvement were going on. The Great Pacific Hotel where a year before I had seen them laying the foundation was now built up, a splendid structure.

I then took the train for St. Louis and arrived at the left bank of the great river about 8 [in the morning]. At that time the bridge was only talked about and so we were taken across to the city on a barge. I visited the Fair which was held that week, and then in the morning went to Kansas City. On the way we had an occasional view of the Missouri. And as there had been a long course of dry weather, the river was so small large stumps and trees were seen lying stranded. The effect of the drought was also seen on the land, where all along the sides of the railway and some of the fields were scorched and burned over.

While on the car I got acquainted with a gentleman from Virginia who was on his way to Kansas City to see friends and do some business. I found him very communicative and he felt a special interest in talking about Scotland. We reached the city about 8 o'clock, had supper at the hotel and had a double bedroom where we spent a good night. Next morning we had a walk out toward the river, saw them leveling down hills for building purposes, [and] walked across the river on a bridge where there was a [gorge]. He pointed out a range of space that he was offered five thousand dollars for, and now the same property today could not be bought for half a million dollars.

That afternoon I took the train for Lawrence, Kansas. Major Ransom whom I had formerly known in Kalamazoo and had gotten Evergreen trees from me, and also recommended me to others, was urged to be his guest while I remained in the place. I thus spent part of two days looking round and had some excursions on the railroad with him. Lawrence, I now found to be a thriving town; having risen from its ashes at the great raid at the beginning of the War.

On the Sabbath I went to the Presbyterian Church and heard a good sermon. I then waited on the Sabbath School and was introduced to a large adult class where I had a hearty reception of Christian intercourse.

I can well recollect that Sabbath evening how the wind blew, little knowing at that time that this was the beginning of the great fire of Chicago. In the morning I took the train to Leavenworth, when I arrived there the telegram had come that Chicago was all ablaze and would soon be wiped out. As it was on my way home I thought I would take a ticket and see the great ruins. I bought a ticket for twenty dollars. This was by the new line just opened and I saw a box of new tickets. I was told that I hoped I would bring good luck to them.

The train did not start till the afternoon, and they gave time to look around the city. We were instructed to go on board a steamer which took us two miles up to a railroad connection. I recollect that here a new bridge was building, but was not yet finished. So after getting on board we traveled all night and came to Museating and Davenport [Iowa] in the morning.

At one of these places we saw the smoldering remains of the great fire. A mill and some other buildings had burnt through the night. We crossed the Mississippi at Rock Island, and here I saw the first car of provisions attached to our train for the destitute of Chicago.

It was here I met with an old Scotsman on the train. He was wondering whether the stockyards would be saved, and he was going up to see, as he had a little interest in them. More provision cars were attached to our train. As we drew nearer we saw and felt the smoke. And in a little while we came to a standstill, all ahead being blocked by cars, and the depot being all burnt.

I walked along on the outside to 22nd Street where the Michigan Central has a station. Here I learned there would be no passenger cars for Kalamazoo till 7 o'clock. I therefore resolved to look round on the desolation till that time. It was with some difficulty that I could get along the streets. I endeavored to see the ruins of some of the places which I had been so much admiring a little more than a week ago, and the contrast was truly sad and sickening. The Great Pacific [Hotel] was now a great heap of smoldering ruins. Some fires were burning fiercely where coal formed, an awful scene of desolation. The water works had been destroyed and this want was being supplied by numerous drays and with barrels selling water for so much per quart or gallon. I noticed some stores outside the burnt district were doing a good trade by selling bread and provisions at enormous high prices. But large stock of provisions were coming in by all the trains, and numerous parties were deputed by city authorities to see that all these were properly doled out. I now drew near to the stations before 7 o'clock and found a vast crowd around the place. Poor people who were going to friends in the country received free pass from the railroads.

We started with a large train and stopped to have supper at

Niles. The table was crowded and then the whistle sounded and there seemed to be no special charge for supper. On arriving at Kalamazoo I found another train alongside just about to start for Chicago. On this were some Kalamazoo people, among which was my brother James and Stephen Cobb. I think they had a carload of provisions. But I found that one great anxiety with my brother was the condition and safety of the stockyards.

I thus got safely home to Kalamazoo again, and then we got the news of great fires in this and other states, especially in the lumber regions. I have never seen so much a dry fall since I came to this country. It has been a matter of wonder how Chicago rose so soon again from its ashes, and I was a witness of this as I visited the city the year after and saw the immense amount of building done and in operation. This is one reason why so many of the buildings are superior and of orderly plan. The fire thus removed all those that were old and unsightly.

* * *

Shortly after this time we found that our Evergreen culture was not so renumerative and the reason was that there was now a great deal more competition. Several of those nurserymen who began with fruit trees now went into raising a great stock of Evergreens. This they did without proper thinning and transplanting. Then having a great stock they must either sell or lose. They sent agents all round to make sales. For a time this was a success, but after a year or two this stock not being transplanted, a great part of it died and thus gave many a disgust at all Evergreen planting. I have every reason to think that some of these parties learned something from the mistakes they had made but it had also the effect of afflicting a great loss upon me.

In raising vegetables we have also found a considerable competition. One great means of success is to have them early, especially is this so with peas, sweet corn, and tomatoes. We have found also that certain of the late vegetables, especially squash and melons can be profitably and successfully grown by a system of alternate cultivation. We have found this especially so in growing our first early peas. These we sow as soon as the season will permit in rows marked about 2 feet apart, leaving every fifth or sixth row vacant. Then sometime about the middle of May when the weather and ground get warm, plant squash in hills along the vacant rows. As soon as they are up they should be hoed about and looked after for bugs. After the crop of peas are gathered about the end of June, have the straw pulled up and the ground well cultivated betwixt the rows of squash, and in a little while they will soon cover the whole ground. In this way we get a large crop of early peas which generally bring a good price and then a full crop of Hubbard squash which are for sale all through the fall and winter. We have always found that squash raised in this way were better than when raised alone. I have found in my experience that this same system of Internal Cultivation can be practiced with many other garden crops.

As my three sons were now all able to do good work, I made up my mind in the fall of 1874 to have another run across the Atlantic and see all the friends in Scotland and England. My wife also thought she had heard too much about Scotland that she would also venture to make the journey along with me. At that time the passages were cheaper than formerly. The agent at Kalamazoo said he could get me a second cabin passage by the Anchor Line for 28 dollars. This I agreed to do with one of their best steamships which was to sail the first week of December. My wife suggested it might be well for us to go by Washington where she had a great many family friends. To this I readily agreed as I had never seen that city or few of her friends. I then proposed to go by way of Cincinnati, where there was a young man of the name of Turnbull from Scotland. His mother was my former wife's sister.

Having made all our arrangements we started from Kalamazoo in the morning about 10 o'clock with the G.R.1. for Cincinnati. This was the day before Thanksgiving, and there was an inch or two of snow on ground. This continued till we came to

Fort Wayne [Indiana] when it disappeared. We arrived at 9 and found James Turnbull waiting for us at the depot. He at once took us to a comfortable room and lodgings, where we had a good supper and were kindly attended by a young lady who in a few weeks later became his wife.

We spent the next day in looking all round the city. A part of it is rising ground, and when the lamps were lighted it brought me a good deal in mind of Old Edinburgh. We also went across on the High Bridge to the Kentucky side and thus had a fine look down on the Ohio below with its numerous shipping craft going up and down. We took a sleeping car for Washington about 8 o'clock and passed a comfortable night. We had breakfast at Wheeling in the morning and had rather an interesting day in passing along the Baltimore and Ohio Road. The hills and tunnels and the varied scenery we passed were something new to me. We lay over two or three hours at one place, and here I met Senator Beck of Kentucky who was on his way to Washington with his wife and daughter. We had a good talk on various subjects, and as he is a Scotsman he felt the more interested when he heard I was going there.

Our ticket was good for another night on the sleeping cart, and about daylight we passed Harper's Ferry [West Virginia]. This place was the more interesting from what I had read of old John Brown and his famous raid. We arrived at the city [Washington] about 9 and took a carriage to the residence of Mr. Mills, my wife's sister's husband. We spent nearly a week in the city, looking all round. At that time they were making some great improvements especially round about the Capitol, taking up some old trees and leveling down the grounds. I visited the Botanical Gardens and got well acquainted with one or two Scotchmen. I also visited the Patent Office and two houses of legislation, the library, and a number of other things. I also ascended the dome of the Capitol and saw people walking like pigmies below and had a fine birds eye view over the whole city. I looked around the White House and adjacent buildings but did not go in. The

Session of the Alabama Claims were then sitting, but I did not go in. I called on our honoured Citizen Judge Wells. I was introduced by some of our friends to an old venerable woman Mrs. Sarah Davis, who had seen every president of the United States. She said that George Washington once kindly laid his hand upon her head. I believe the last she saw was President Hays.

We left Washington on the 5th of December. The vessel with which we had engaged was to sail on the 6th. We had a pleasant and interesting journey in seeing so many places, I had read, such as Baltimore, Philadelphia, and other noted places. And then New Jersey with its vast industrial population verging upon the great city of New York. We reached that place about 4 o'clock and took our lodgings for the night at a hotel near by.

In the morning I went down to the dock and saw the vessel. A great crew of men were loading wheat and barrels of flour. The passengers had orders to be on board with their baggage at 12. At that time we were ready but found them still loading, and this continued until 4 o'clock, when the bell rang and we moved out of the harbor.

There is always considerable confusion at first starting, and as it was beginning to get dark, we were shoved into a berth in the steerage. I was obliged to submit to this till morning, when I spoke to one of the officers that I had a second cabin ticket and wished to have a berth of that sort. From this man I received no satisfactory answer, so I at once went to the Captain and stated my case. He seemed a little imperious and gave me some uncivil language. Then I told him I had crossed the Atlantic several times before and if he did not give me my right, I should give this ship the benefit of an advertisement on both sides when I came to land. He then talked with one of the subordinates who gave me a sign to follow him, when I was shown a comfortable berth for myself and wife. Our provisions were there served to us and we had some fine neighbor associates.

We had only a very short qualm of sea sickness and the weather was for the most part so favourable that we could often remain hours on deck and see the great billows heave and swell. Our vessel went by the north of Ireland, and we came in sight of land in the forenoon and ran into the bay of Moville in the evening, where some of our passengers left. In the morning we were in Greenock Harbour, where were some custom inspections. It was put to our option either to remain on the vessel for 3 hours till the tide would permit to go up to Glasgow or we could now leave and take the first train. This we did and had a good view of the scenery by the way through. There was a considerable amount of fog and smoke, and this was more apparent when we came near Paisley, and from there to Glasgow where factory chimneys are one of the prominent features of the landscape. We then had a scramble for our trunk and then got a hack which took us to the Cobden Hotel. We stopped there for two days looking round up the great sights of the city. There had been a fall of snow and a considerable frost, and what with clouds and smoke, we had never seen the sun since we landed.

I had sent a letter to Andrew Stevenson letting him know that we would be at Edinburgh with the morning train from Glasgow. So we started and after traveling about ten miles we got some little glimpses of the sun. There is some fine farming land on this line, and we noticed some large fields of the finest turnips. In approaching Edinburgh from the west the Castle and Arthur's Seat are among the first prominent objects that meets the eye. The old town on the right and the new on the left are altogether a great contrast.

* * *

We found our friend Andrew waiting for us at the depot where we had a cordial reception. We engaged a hack which took us and our trunk over to Bristo Street where he then stopped with [his] mother. It was now about the 20th of December, our sea passage being a little over ten days. I had a happy meeting with John Brown and some old acquaintance, but there were some that had passed away since the last in this city in 12 years before. My wife did not feel well for some time and had to keep to the house for two or three weeks.

After being a day or two in the city I took a run out to Kelso and Jedburgh to see the friends, but there were some I could not see, as both my sisters, Agnes Huggan and Margaret Telfer were dead. I also went to Burnfoot and saw brother Alexander and his family. I also saw George and William Purvis. At that time William was the president of the famous club that was in the way of meeting on the first Friday of each month, where they had dinner in the Cross Keys Hotel and then a talk afterwards on their various experiences in farming. He was very anxious that I should meet with so many of the farmers of the district with which I was formerly so well acquainted. I said I would endeavor to do so. In the mean time I went back to Edinburgh, as my brother John was expected from Nottingham. That night when I went in, my brother John arrived and we had a happy meeting. I think it was the next day after dinner that John Brown called at my sister's house to see me and brother John.

After talking a little, my brother expressed a wish to take a walk out and see Downie and Lairs Greenhouses, these being considered at that time the finest in the city. These were situated at the west end near to Donaldson[']s Hospital. So we walked in that direction, remarking as [we] went upon the many improvements that were being made. In a little time we came to the range of greenhouses. There was an extra large one in front which seemed as a place of reception, for here we found a number of ladies walking about and admiring the various specimens of flowering plants.

I noticed their foreman going about and cutting a bouquet of flowers for some ladies. After he had finished, I went to speak with him. When looking full at me he said, "Oh, Mr. Taylor, is it you?" "Well," I said, "I think I recognize your face but can't recollect when or where." "Why," said he, "do you not recollect your old apprentice, Andrew Kier?" Then I recollect that this was one of the young men that served his time with me while I was fore-man in the Kelso Nursery. I then introduced my brother and John Brown, mentioning how I was now on a visit to friends in this place. Brown then said to Kier, "So you were an apprentice with Mr. Taylor. He also taught me to be a gardener when I was Mr. Yair's boy at Eckford Manse. But," said John in a warm way, "he taught me something far better—to be a Christian."

Kier then looked him in the face and said, "This sir, was one of the first things he taught me, and he knows how I became a member of the Church in Kelso."

At this my brother John came forward in a smiling way and said, "I am afraid we will now make him too proud of himself for he also taught me to be a gardener and after that a Christian."

I here learned a lesson that in our ordinary business of life, if we are Christians we will be workers together with God, and that we can make known the truth of the gospel to our fellow men while working with our hands. This testimony which I had from these three witnesses was a strong attestation to this fact and goes to show how much everyone had in their power to influence others for either good or evil. It is a solemn thing to live.

The new year had come in and I thought I would take a run out to Kelso, as I had promised, to meet with Mr. Purvis at the Farmer's Club. I therefore started on the morning train, though it was blowing and snowing pretty hard I had no fear of getting along. After passing Dalkeith, the storm seemed to increase and as we came on higher ground, great snow drifts were being laid in and in a little time our train had to stop. We thus remained standing for a few minutes. We learned that the early train that had gone out before was stuck in the snow drift before us. On looking out we saw the passengers of that train coming tumbling and plodding through the snow in order to get aboard ours. In a little while this was accomplished and our cars were crowded with a sorry looking company. Our train then put back and took us again to Edinburgh where on presenting our tickets we received our money.

I wrote a letter to Mr. Purvis stating what had prevented me from coming to his club meeting, and he wrote me how he had been prevented in having stuck with his carriage on the way to Kelso. There would be no meeting until the first Friday in February. I thus spent a few more days in Edinburgh and once more visited the top of Arthur's Seat.

After my wife had gained strength, we went out and visited our friends at Jedburgh and Burnfoot, and when at Kelso boarded with Mr. Thomas Sleight of the Temperance Hotel. I had now made arrangements to visit London and our niece Isabella Turnbull at Tunbridge Wells. I therefore went by the way of Berwick where I met my old friend, Mr. Matthew Young, of the [Linseed] Oil Cake Factory, and spent a good part of the day with him and his family. We then took the train in the evening for Newcastle, arrived there and had lodgings at a hotel. Went out in the morning and saw the great sheep and cattle market, called on Mr. Thomas Rutherford who formerly kept the Temperance Hotel at Kelso. And then with him I found the Rev. John Rutherford who was the minister of the Evangelical Union Church when I first came to Kelso.

We then went down to Hartlepool and spent a night with our nephew, Thomas Turnbull and his family. We then took the train to London and arrived there in the afternoon. The first night we stopped at a hotel near the station. And when we went for our trunk we experienced an act of civility from the railway porter, who carried it free of charge to the hotel. Next day we went down to the centre of the city and took lodgings at what is called the Beanford Building, adjacent to the Strand. Here I think we spent about ten days looking round the great city. We took the run down to our niece and her mother at Tunbridge Wells. This is a great summer watering place and we spent a day and a night looking round. We visited the Crystal Place at Sydenham where nearly all the world is represented in a pictorial way. We took one day to visit the Royal Gardens at Kew.

The curator of Kew Gardens proved to be the man who was

foreman at the Duke of Roxburgh Garden when I was with Stuart and Mein at Kelso. We had a pleasant chat. He then said we were at liberty to walk all through the various greenhouses and grounds. There is a large palm house where these are grown to full size, and in the other houses all the tropical plants and every variety of plant and flower of the world.

Among the notable things we visited in London was the Tower, Westminster Abb[e]y, and the Houses of Parliament, Madame T[us]sauds; these and many others I had visited before but they were all new to my wife, and I often enjoy these things more the second time.

We left London in the morning by the western route, lay over at Carlisle for an hour or two and arrived at Newto[w]n Station in the evening. In the morning I took a walk across the Tweed to Dryburgh Abb[e]y, saw the grave of Sir Walter Scott, and then made a call on (brother and sister) Major and Lady [Grizell Baillie],[12] who lived adjacent to the Abb[e]y. The object of this call was to know about Mr. Robert Renwick who had died since I was last in Scotland.

We made another visit to our friends at Jedburgh and Burnfoot. And one day while there I thought I would like to visit the old ground where I lived from five to fourteen years of age. I therefore went over by the top of Linton Hill, where I had a good birds eye view of all the old ground. Then I went down the moor by the celebrated spot where tradition says a great monster worm or snake once existed which swallowed up every living thing that came near. This is a narrow deep glen called Wormington where this monster existed. I recollect of seeing an old picture on the old Linton Church door which represented a man on horseback riding at full speed with a great long fiery torch in his hand and thrusting it into the gaping mouth of this monster, by which means it was killed. And hence came the verse, "The daft Laird of Larristone He Killed the Worme of Wormiston and was a Lonton Parochine." This I suppose had its origin from St. George and the Dragon.[13]

* * *

I went down across the Yetholm road to the mansion of Old Graden, now the property of a Mr. Humble, whom I formerly knew in Kelso. I called and was kindly received and pressed to stay to dinner. I then went over the hill to the east and then down a long strip of pasture land on the south side of Hoselaw [Moss] which we used to call Cakes Shott. I was now alongside of the [Moss] where I used to gather cranberries and sometimes seek wild duck and snipe nests. Then I came near the east end of the [Moss] and crossed once more the little brook that drains it. I found that they had made a deep cut down the centre of this [moss] and sheep and cattle were now pasturing where I had sometimes seen them drowned.

I then went up with the [Moss] on my left hand to the site of the old Farm Lochinches where my Father lived for five years when a shepherd at Hos[e]law Bank. The old place is now all down and a little square plantation now occupies the site. I went to the spot where our garden used to be and a little farther to the west on the verge of the [Moss] to see the old spring well, where I had carried many hundred pails of water. It was still bubbling and springing up. Then I went round to the Lo[c]h and the little island where I used to gather baskets of Pickmaw eggs. I found however that the cut down through the [Moss] had lowered the water in this lo[c]h considerably.

Thus far I had seen no person but was left to my own meditations. Where was now Father and Mother and many other friends that we used to meet with and be so familiar? It was a grand lesson to me of the mutibility of all earthly things. As I went round toward the east side of the Lo[c]h I saw a man plowing, I went and talked with him. I asked about the present proprietors and if he ever heard or knew of certain parties that once farmed this land, but he said he did not. Here was the Lo[c]h and the large [moss], and other external features, but the people who were once the active agents had all passed away. I went around the east end of the Lo[c]h where so often I had helped at sheep washings, then up the road to the high ridge of the Hos[e]law Bank. Here I had a fine look to Berwickshire to the northeast and to the old Hume Castle and other prominent objects to the westward. In the foreground was the old village of Lempitlaw where I first went to school. And the various fields and farmhouses seemed as familiar. I looked at the farm homestead of Hos[e]law Bank. The old houses were nearly all down. The only one now standing which I had known so well was being used as a Blacksmith Shop.

Going a little to the west I went up the old road where I first went to school, to the top of Graden Hill where I had again another view of the old familiar ground. I then took a road west to the garden when my father was shepherd two years with the proprieter, a Mr. William Dawson, an uncle of James Dawson who was the first editor of the *Kelso Chronicle* in 1832. I found some changes had taken place on the buildings of this farm, but some of the old trees were yet standing. As I came westward I saw that they had nearly cut down the fir plantation which was the first I ever saw planted, and was pointed out to me by my grandmother when I was accompanying her from our house to her home in Morebattle.

I then passed the farm of Gre[e]nle[e]s which I had done hundreds of times on my way to Linton School, then I passed the farm of Bankhead and then past the old Linton School. Here I called on John Young who was Blacksmith here, with whom I got well acquainted when at Ormiston. I had thus spent a most interesting day with the old familiar scenes of the past. I think it preached me a sermon from which I derived great profit.

While at Burnfoot I made some calls over to Morebattle where were some few old acquaintances, but how few, if any, when I first saw that village with my grandmother about 70 years ago. We now bade goodbye to our friends at Burnfoot and Mr. Purvis very kindly sent his man with his carriage to take us to [Kirk-bank] Station. On our way we called at Marlefield where I used to work the garden, and there we met with Miss Johnstone, a

10. Gravestone, Eckford Parish Church, marking the burial site of George Taylor's mother and father and his brother John.

SOURCE: JIM HIGGINS

good Christian lady with whom I was formerly well acquainted. We then drove to [Kale] Waterfoot, and left our carriage and walked up the road to Eckford Church Yard specially to visit the plot of ground where the bodies of my Father, Mother, and first wife, Helen Robson with her two infant boys are buried. After looking round the old Church we took a walk up to the manse to make a call on Rev. Joseph Yair and his wife, where we were very kindly received. After a pleasant talk we then took our way by the Chain Bridge and down the road by Ormiston Mill to the station at Kirkbank, where we took the train to Jedburgh and there remained a few days with the Huggans.

One of these days with my wife I took a walk up the Jed Water to visit some of the old romantic and once familiar scenes. Among these were specially the two famous Oak Trees known for hundreds of years by the names of the Kings of the Wood, and the [Capon] Trees, the first for its majestic straight tall [trunk?], and the other for its division into branches at the bottom where it extends for a great breadth on all sides. We also visited the old Cathedral [Abbey] and its surroundings and got photographs of them. One day we took a drive round the country with a horse and gig. We first went by our friends at Bonjedward and then by way of the Ancrum Bridge where we made a call on James Weaver who was for many years Forrester to the Marquis of Lothian, and then up by the village of Ancrum. Then calling on another acquaintance and then we took the nearest and best way to the village of Lilliesleaf where Charlotte, Jean Whilleans [Whellans?] youngest sister, was living and married with a family. After spending a few hours with them we took the straight road across the Teviot to Denholm. Then direct for Jedburgh up and along the north side of the Dunion where there is a most extended view on every side, then down hill pass the Jail to the old Burgh.

That evening we had engaged to have tea and supper with late Provost William Deans and his wife, where we spent some happy hours. I spent one day mostly on foot on the way from Jedburgh to Kelso looking at some of the old familiar places. I came by the way of Crailing, making a call on the Rev. Adam Cunningham, and likewise on John [Dodds], the old Blacksmith. He was now retired from business and very feeble, but seemed to have pleasure in talking of old things.

I came down by the Crailing Tofts, there calling on Walter Rutherford the farmer, then down the road to the Burn Houses where I lived for four years, but now they are no more, there being only a plowed field where the five houses and gardens once stood. I next came down and cross the Chain Bridge and down the side of the Teviot to where was a fine hardwood plantation which I had thinned and pruned up about 35 years ago. I was much gratified to see what a proper system of forestry can accomplish in a few years. I then walked down to Roxburgh and took the train to Kelso.

My wife came down the next day when shortly after we went to Edinburgh and then in due time, when our ship was to sail we came to Glasgow. Here we were detained a day or two longer then the time specified, as the vessel had struck [an] iceberg in coming over and had to undergo repairs.

Both my wife and myself had a little touch of seasickness for the first two days but soon got all right. There was a little sensation on board one afternoon which was only known to a few at that time. I was walking on deck when all at once a report came from below that the ship was on fire. In some way a pile of coals had caught fire. The Captain was called and there was a hurry among the seamen. I noticed one or two of the men were pulling off a hatch cover in order I supposed to pour down water, when all at once the Captain almost struck them down. The reason for this was that if the air had got access, the whole would soon have been ablaze. Then it was that some windlass and ropes were applied in another direction and I was called on to pull and assist. In a few minutes it was announced that the fire was subdued and all danger was over.

There was no doubt this was an inferior vessel. As after we were more than half way over one of the boilers gave out and the remainder of the voyage had to be accomplished with one, which made it very slow work, making our whole voyage nearly 20 days.

I had a box with nursery stock on board and had again some trouble in getting it through the custom house. After this we started for Delhi to see our cousins, the Mables, and with some roundabouts and delays we arrived there about the first or second of April. We spent three or four pleasant days with them and were introduced to a good many Scotchmen. We then came by the way of Niagara Falls and Canada and spent a few hours with Tom Huggan and his family at Paris [Michigan]. Then on to Detroit and arrived at Kalamazoo on the evening of the 6th of April.

* * *

We had altogether a pleasant excursion, but I learned one thing that I can travel a great deal cheaper when alone than when I am accompanied with a lady.

Since 1875 I have gone through a varied experience in the country. Up till 1880 the nursery was run in my name and on my account paying all the wages for labor, taxes, and household expenses. My son James ran the vegetable department. But the old mortgage was hanging over me and a crisis came, when in the spring of 1881 Mr. Breese in the form of a legal process foreclosed that mortgage and then things came to a sort of standstill with me. I made a Christian protest against this to Mr. Breese as an act of injustice in the sight of God. I showed him that after paying my brother Andrew's passage in 1836 that I gave him 100 dollars with instructions to have it laid out in land (either by himself or brother James) in Kalamazoo suitable for nursery and garden purposes. This I showed him with the note to this effect with Andrew's signature. I therefore appealed against this case being settled according to the Civil Laws of Michigan but rather by Christian Jury to be chosen by neutral parties and then submitting to them the whole facts of the case from the beginning. This he refused to do and therefore I consider he violated both the Law of Equity and the Law of Christ. I was a little troubled [in] the course of my life, that after [I had] done so much for the welfare of my brothers and sisters and my own family, that I had been thus entrapped to be left in comparative poverty and dependence in my old age. With this feeling I cast my care upon God and looked to Him for help, and I have great reason as I look back to see that his good hand has been over me this far, and that this case, though looking dark at first, will yet be among the all things that has been working in some unseen way for my greatest ultimate good.

It was here that my son James came in to pay a certain amount of the debt and took the responsibility and has paid all up since. The place is now his and I work pretty hard through the spring and summer. I have a comfortable home with my wife, good bed and board, and have always a little money on hand for Church expenses and for 5 or 6 of the best papers which keeps me properly posted with what is going on in the civil and religious world.

The only property that I now have is the two acres of orchard on the College Addition which I expect to sell some of these days for 2,000 dollars.

I now come to notice some of the events connected with my family and friends. My oldest daughter Isabella was married in the fall of 1870 to Romulo E. Bangs, who was my wife's cousin and who with his brother has a large farm in Modesto, California. They have now in 1887 a family of six children.

My youngest daughter Violet, being in poor health went out to stay with her sister in 1876, her health greatly improved for some time, but later she was affected with some internal disease, of which she died in 1886.

My brother Alexander who for a great many years was steward with William Purvis at Linton Burnfoot died about 8 years ago. His widow with some of the family are now living at Sprouston on the Tweed near Kelso. He died in November 1879.

Here also in Kalamazoo death has been doing its work among our relations. My brother James's wife, Helen Gilkerson died June 29, 1881 and also James rather suddenly on December 25, 1881. The last death in my own family relation was my oldest sister Mary, in Edinburgh, whose death took place there on the 16th day of May 1877. Thus leaving only two out of a family of eight—myself the oldest born in 1803 and John the youngest now in Nottingham, England, born in 1821.

I now come to give some account of what I have been doing in Michigan lately. And I may mention that I became a life member of the Michigan Horticultural Society about 1875. The sum of 10 dollars entitled me to the privilege. Since that time I have frequently been in the way of taking part in the various meetings. The most prominent of these has been on the subject of hedging and forestry. These have appeared in the Annual Reports of the Society. The first of these was read by me at the winter meeting which was held in Paw Paw, [V]an Buren County [Michigan]. It was entitled *Arboriculture and Forestry*, and printed in the 8th Annual Report at page 193. The second article is on forestry at page 68 of the 9th volume, and another the same year on hedging, page 153 of the same.

All these were not a matter of theory with me [but] what I had both seen and practiced. The last time that I spoke on this subject was at a meeting of the State Forestry Commission held at Grand Rapids on the 26th and 27th of January 1888. At this meeting there was a great deal of talk about the necessity of planting, but no practical mode as to the way by which it could be done. I urged upon this meeting that such a display in all its bearings and relations should at once be done, showing the people that it could be done and the way to do it.

Since my visit to Scotland and England in 1874 and 1875, I have not traveled a great way from home. About 1878 I took advantage of an excursion to Petaskey and Mack[i]nac Island [Michigan], and I felt a good deal interested in passing through the north woods to see the way in which many of these were being wasted and destroyed.

I saw some places where great fires had recently swept through for miles and I soon perceived the reason for this. I observed certain places where timber had been cut that a great amount of brush and heavy branches were lying in piles so promiscuously scattered that a fire once started with a little wind would soon make a general conflagration. This destructive waste might all be prevented by having this brush collected and burnt before the hot dry weather came on.

I spent a part of two days on Mack[i]nac Island seeking some of nature's great wonders and also collecting a good many young Evergreen seedlings which I found growing abundantly under the shade of certain large trees.

I have also been in the way at several times in making a run through to Chicago and St. Louis and observed how both these cities are growing and advancing. After looking at these in their various relations, we can then form some more correct opinions of this great country.

There is another thing that we can see in these and other cities and that supplying the sources from which so much sin and misery and crime originates. Most conspicuous of these is the many and various saloons with their sources of supply the breweries and distilleries. It is here that an impartial observer perceived a great anomoly in our government. Special business is to punish and repress crime, but while it seems to be doing this with one hand, it is with the other fostering and encouraging it by granting license to sell those ingredients which are the most prolific of all crimes.

In all these cities we see a great many fine churches, but these saloons and drinking places are a sort of Devil's agent that work right against them. These churches all have Sabbath Schools with teachers laboring to instruct and praying that their scholars may be brought up in the nurture and admonition of the Lord. Here these Christian citizens are sowing the good seed of the word, while they suffer an enemy to be in the same field sowing the tares which so readily grow, so that the good seed has a great struggle for existence. From this I infer that every Christian is a warrior and should put on the whole armor of God and also being an American Citizen he ought to use this ballot to strike down the Distillery, the Saloon, and the law of license. In this way only will every Christian be consistent in following up their prayers by their works.

Through the course of the spring and summer of 1888 there was nothing that occurred of any note different from the usual events of daily life.

In the fall I took advantage of an excursion given to Chicago which I had not seen for four years. I spent a part of three days looking around the city and a good part of one at the stockyards. And on going to these grounds I found one advantage which did not exist a few years ago and that was the cable cars. These now run through all the principal streets of the city and I thus took one from Madison Street where I lodged to the stockyards nearly 4 miles for the sum of 5 cents. I had previously learned that a Mr. Clay a Scotchman had a business office at these grounds and having got his address I called at the office and found him. This Mr. Clay is a son of John Clay, who has long been a farmer on the farm of Kerchester in Sprouston Parish.

* * *

After an introduction and where I was from and that I was a Scotchman who had spent the best of my life in Kelso and neighborhood, I at once received a very cordial reception. He then said that owing to the amount of business he was sorry he could not [go] round with me, but he went out and pointed to me where I could best walk and see some of the greatest sights of the various stock pens of these yards and buildings.

I found on looking round that the grounds and buildings had been greatly enlarged and improved since I had last seen them. There is now a high walk where you can walk around and look down on the various departments of stock penned up for slaughter. And there are certain places where you can see this process going on, and where it is now in great measure done by machinery.

In the centre of these yards and on the outside are hundreds of railway cars bringing in live stock and shipping away the slaughtered meat to all parts of the country. In the summer this is mostly done in refrigerated cars.

It is only as we look at the vast amount of stock that is constantly being brought in here that we get some little idea of the resources and extent of country that keeps up this constant supply. There are also other cities in the west [such] as St. Louis and Kansas City that have now extensive stockyards and are [e]very year increasing.

I spent another day in the northwest part of the city, went out to Graceland where is the great cemetary and the extensive grounds so tastefully laid out. Then I came in by way of Lincoln Park where great improvements are still being made in walks and drives, and especially a broad boulevard all along the side of the lake for nearly two miles.

I came in by the great building where the motive power is originated for driving cable cars, which is one of our great modern inventions. I saw some very high new buildings which are being put up in various parts of the city, and all around the suburbs it is extending in every direction.

The year 1888 closed with us in much the usual way and shortly after the new year in 1889 my wife made a visit to Schoolcraft to see her sister and family for a few days. It was shortly after she came home that she was seized with some disease in the throat which gave her a great deal of trouble, so much that we sent for a doctor who put her under a course of medicine. All through a part of February when it was thought that this throat trouble was nearly resolved. But all at once she was suddenly seized with some internal trouble affecting the heart and lungs, by which she was so prostrated that after this she could scarcely ever speak and no medicine seemed to give any relief. She did not seem to suffer much pain but gradually got weaker and on the 5th of March she passed away as in a sleep without any sensation of pain. Both her sisters, Mrs. Jack of St. Louis and Mrs. Bow of Schoolcraft were with her at the time.

The funeral was held on Friday the 8th from the house to the Mountain Home Cemetery, a good company of friends and neighbors attending. The Rev. Mr. Jones of the Episcopal Church, her minister and the Rev. Mr. Lobe of the Presbyterian Church performed the religious exercises.

I was thus left for the fourth time a widower, and I now felt that I had lost one of my best friends.

My son James is now keeping house with a hired woman and I have reason to thank God that I do not want for any of the comforts of life and that my health is good and that I have still strength to do a considerable amount of work. I have as usual dressed all our evergreen and ornamental hedges and also some others in the city.

The only excursion I have made this year was to the Great Exhibition at Detroit in the month of September. I had not seen that city for the last eight years. I found it greatly advanced and still growing. The exhibition I found altogether to be a great thing with certain features I had never seen before.

I had some fine steamboat rides up and down the great river and it is only in this way that you can see some of the great business industries of this city. In one of these I visited Belisle Park where some great improvements are being made. A great many sailing vessels of all sorts are constantly going up and down this river and shows that a vast amount of business is done betwixt the east and west. After looking round the city for three days I again arrived safely home at Kalamazoo.

We have had a course of very dry weather this fall but the first fruits of winter has come upon very suddenly, as on the 26th of November snow fell from 10 to 12 inches, so that on the 28th, Thanksgiving Day, we had fine sleighing.

According to the usual custom the various Churches in the city united in holding religious services in the first Baptist Church.

Death of Nurseryman First to Market Celery Here Recorded in Gazette of August 30, 1891.

The death of Kalamazoo's veteran nurseryman was recorded in The Gazette of Aug. 30, 1891, as occurring on the previous date. He was George Taylor, for many years a prominent resident of the city and a native of Scotland. The data concerning Mr. Taylor is reprinted in the following:

"Mr. George Taylor, veteran nurseryman and prominent old resident, was found dead in his room Sunday morning. Death resulted either from fainting or the bursting of a blood vessel. He complained of feeling badly last Monday and Dr. Snook had been attending him for a week. Friday, he seemed to feel better.

"Mr. Taylor was born at Hannan, Roxburghshire, Scotland, Feb. 12, 1803. He was first a shepherd and afterward became superintendent of the Stuart and Mein Nursery, established at Kelso, Scotland. He came to Kalamazoo, where his brothers, James and Andrew, were prominent business men, in 1855. He brought with him a large nursery stock of ornamental trees, evergreens, and flower plants and established a nursery at the west end of town in the region of Henderson park. Many of the large shade trees in the city were planted by him. In 1856 he grew the first celery for market and supplied the markets and adjacent towns with celery for 10 years. He continued in business at the west end until 1867, when he purchased a place in Portage street, where he lived with his son, James A. Taylor. In 1881 he retired from active business and sold out to his son.

"He also had great literary talent, and in a contest for the best essay on the cause of a disease which was destroying the potatoes of Scotland in 1844, he won a gold medal offered by the Royal Agricultural Society. In 1875 he revisited Scotland. He always did considerable writing. He was president of the Burns Society of this city.

"Mr. Taylor has been an active member of the First Presbyterian church ever since he has resided here."

11. Reprinted obituary of George Taylor from a Michigan publication.

SOURCE: GEORGE REYNOLDS II

NOTES

1 The site of the Caverton Edge Race Course is now the Bowmont Forest, which used to be the largest race-course in Scotland.

2 This quotation is from the poem 'The Holy Fair' by Robert Burns. The actual words are, 'Here farmers gash, in ridin graith, Gaed hoddin by their cotters.'

3 The sign read, 'Humpty dumpty, heerie, peerie, Step in here and ye'll be cheerie. Try oor speerits an' oor porter, They'll make the road aa the shorter, And if ye hae a mind tae stay, Your horse could get good corn and hay.'

4 The Wren's Nest in Jedburgh was one of the first boarding schools in Scotland, founded in 1820 by Rev. Alexander Burnett.

5 'Not pressed the nipple, strangled in life's porch. Here is the mother, with her sons and daughters; The barren wife; the long demurring maid.', from 'The Grave' by Robert Blair.

6 Newton Don is a mansion house near Kelso.

7 The Game Laws were a conten-tious and politically sensitive cause for much of the mid-19th century, finally being repealed in 1886.

8 This line in the poem is 'whare in the snow the chapman smoor'd'; unclear where the 'Kinaves' comes from, as it is not in the poem.

9 Robert Heron, his family and an apprentice are in the 1851 Eckford census.

10 The *Alabama* was built at Birken-head and used during the American Civil War by the Confederate Navy to attack ships of the Union States. After the war the American Govern-ment sued the UK Government for compensation for losses caused by the actions of the *Alabama*.

11 Mrs Robertson, *née* Margaretta Miller, was the wife of John Robert-son, a wealthy London merchant, and daughter of a Royal Navy com-mander. Her sister's son Robert Shedden also went to sea. In his own schooner *Nancy Dawson*, he offered to help in the search for Sir John Franklin in 1849, even though he had consumption. He died aged 29. In memory of her nephew, Mrs Robertson gave Shedden Park to the town of Kelso. See A. Mitchell: *A. James Dickson and his Legacy,* Kelso: *c.*1997.

12 Lady Grizell Baillie was the youngest child of George Baillie of Mellerstain House. She was the first deaconess to be appointed to the Church of Scotland.

13 From Linton Kirk, Morebattle. 'This sculptured Tympanum, known as the Somerville Stone is a "notable remain" practically unique in Scotland and it is one of the finest examples of its kind. Legend affirms that it depicts John Somerville killing a monster which by its breath was able to draw the flocks and herds around it within reach of its fangs.' For this exploit it is said William the Lion conferred upon him the lands of Linton; 'The wode Laird of Laristone/ Slew the Worme of Wormiston / And wan a' Linton Parochine.' Thanks to Mr Bert Adams for this information.

GLOSSARY

This selective list contains only those terms found in the text that may need explanation.

bandwin, a band of three to eight reapers served by one bandster.

cadger, used in Scots as in standard English to mean a travelling hawker (chiefly of fish), or beggar. Also has the following peculiarly Scots usage, a person of disagreeable temper.

caul, a weir or dam to divert water for a mill.

cotter, or **cottar**, older meaning: farm tenant who occupied a cottage with or without a piece of land attached, the farmer working the cottar's land in return for services rendered; a peasant who occupied a cottage and rented a small plot of land from a landlord. Now applied to a married dependant on a farm with a cottage as part of contract.

creel, a large wicker basket, frequently one of a pair used for holding articles carried on horseback; also, a wooden crate or box for similar use.

darg, a day's work, specially of harvest-work; a quantity (of turf, peats, or hay) representing a day's work; an extent (of meadow) which can be mowed in a day.

elder, one who is elected and ordained in the Presbyterian church to the exercise of government in ecclesiastical courts, without having authority to teach.

flitting, articles or goods removed or carried; removal of a thing or person from one place to another; removing to another place of residence.

guinea, English gold coin, not coined since 1813, first struck in 1663 with the nominal value of 20s., but from 1717 until its disappearance circulating as legal tender at the rate of 21s. Sum of money equal to the value of this coin. In present use, a name for the sum of £1.05 (21s).

hind, servant; especially, in later use, a farm servant, an agricultural labourer.

packman, itinerant trader who carries goods in a pack for sale; a pedlar.

pick maw, black-headed gull, *Larus ridibundus*. Formerly also: a tern (genus *Sterna*)

precentor, precentor or person appointed to lead congregational singing.

rod, a stick, six ells in length, used for taking measurements (an ell is c.37 inches in length).

sarking, length of (chiefly or only linen) cloth sufficient to make one 'sark' (shift or shirt).

Sustentation Fund, money collected at a local level, put into a central fund and then the income divided amongst the ministers of the Free Church of Scotland who would each receive an equal dividend.

swingling, to dress flax by beating in the process of linen manufacture.

synod, body of ministers and elders constituting the church court intermediate between Presbytery and General Assembly, or particular meeting of such a body.

term, one of the four days of the year legally marking the falling-due of certain payments, such as rents, wages, *etc.*, the settlement of business accounts, commencement and expiry of leases, and of contracts of employment, especially on farms.

waterbrash, spontaneous flooding of the mouth with a clear, slightly salty fluid, symptom commonly accompanies upper gastrointestinal distress such as heartburn, peptic ulcer disease and even acute gastroenteritis.

wynd, narrow street, lane or alley, leading off a main thoroughfare in a town and frequently following a sinuous or curving course.

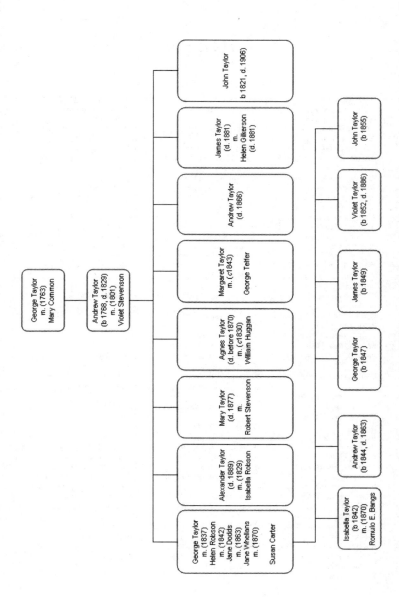

George Taylor
m. (1763)
Mary Common

Andrew Taylor
(b 1768, d. 1829)
m. (1801)
Violet Stevenson

George Taylor
m. (1837)
Helen Robson
m. (1842)
Jane Dodds
m. (1863)
Jane Whellans
m. (1870)
Susan Carter

Alexander Taylor
(d. 1889)
m. (1829)
Isabella Robson

Mary Taylor
(d. 1877)
m.
Robert Stevenson

Agnes Taylor
(d. before 1870)
m. (c1830)
William Huggan

Margaret Taylor
(c1843)
m.
George Telfer

Andrew Taylor
(d. 1866)

James Taylor
(d. 1881)
m.
Helen Glikerson
(d. 1881)

John Taylor
b 1821, d. 1906)

Isabella Taylor
(b 1842)
m. (1870)
Romulo E. Bangs

Andrew Taylor
(b 1844, d. 1863)

George Taylor
(b 1847)

James Taylor
(b 1849)

Violet Taylor
(b 1852, d. 1886)

John Taylor
(b 1855)

INDEX

174